5 I/O
75¢

BI 0346

SPENSER'S DEFENSE OF LORD GREY

AMS PRESS
NEW YORK

SPENSER'S DEFENSE OF LORD GREY

By

H. S. V. JONES

UNIVERSITY OF ILLINOIS
1919

Library of Congress Cataloging in Publication Data

Jones, Harry Stuart Vedder, 1878-1942.
  Spenser's defense of Lord Grey.

  Reprint of the 1919 ed. published by University of
Illinois, Urbana, which was issued as v. 5, no. 3 of
University of Illinois studies in language and literature.
  Includes bibliographical references.
  1. Spenser, Edmund, 1552?-1599. 2. Grey de Wilton,
Arthur Grey, 14th baron, 1536-1593. 3. Irish question.
I. Title. II. Series: Illinois. University. Illinois
studies in language and literature ; v. 5, no. 3.
PR2364.J55   1976   821'.3 (B)   73-170822
ISBN 0-404-03599-X

Reprinted from the edition of 1919, Urbana
First AMS edition published in 1976
Manufactured in the United States of America

AMS PRESS INC.
NEW YORK, N. Y. 10003

PREFACE

It should not be necessary to say that the author of this monograph holds no brief for England's Irish policy in the sixteenth century. Nor has he undertaken to defend against all comers a body of political opinion which, while manifestly congenial to the eclectic genius of Spenser, nevertheless fell far short of a satisfactorily integrated system of ideas. In its primary intention, indeed, the study is descriptive rather than argumentative, even though the necessity of defending the position here taken has led to the adoption of a mildly controversial manner. The larger questions of criticism which will occur to the mind of the judicious reader I have not attempted to answer, in the belief that these might be profitably deferred until after the publication of studies complementary to the one here offered had laid a broader foundation for an estimate of Spenser's position in the literature of the English Renaissance.

For the loan of books I am indebted to the libraries of Harvard, Yale, the University of Chicago, and the University of Cincinnati; and for suggestions and criticisms of various kinds to Professor E. B. Greene, Professor A. S. Pease, and the editorial staff of the University Studies.

H. S. V. J.

TABLE OF CONTENTS

CHAPTER I.	Spenser, Lord Grey, and Ireland...	7
CHAPTER II.	The Cult of Nationalism and Tolerance in England and France..	16
CHAPTER III.	Spenser and *les Politiques*...	48
CHAPTER IV.	Spenser and Machiavelli	64

CHAPTER I
SPENSER, LORD GREY, AND IRELAND

Among poets in exile who have made contribution to the literature of melancholy, a secure place should be reserved for Joachim du Bellay. In the flute-like melodies of the *Regrets* we hear as clear a romantic note as the period has to offer, answering in key and pitch to a genuine *mal du pays*. The revolt in the famous sonnet series against the cult of humanism loses none of its interest from the circumstance that it was composed and in large measure written in the eternal city. We can read the promise of a later day in the glance of Du Bellay averted from the Roman marbles to the grey cottages of Anjou. Furthermore, his verse speaks the language of ordinary men; it is made without art. No longer is the poet concerned with lofty themes and the colors of rhetoric; rather he laughs and weeps with his verses, making them, as he says, the secretaries of his heart. In a word, du Bellay is here writing what one of his French critics has called *un journal intime*.[1]

Passing over the satiric mood of this *journal intime*, which brings into focus the brilliant frivolities and the inner corruption of the City of the Popes, I turn to an exile who is even more celebrated than his French contemporary, and whose lot was cast in very different places. In the orchestration of Edmund Spenser one also hears the flute complaining, but though there is much that is autobiographical there is little of the *journal intime* in *Mother Hubbard's Tale* or *Colin Clout*. Here and there in Spenser's poetry, however, as in certain dedicatory sonnets of the *Faerie Queene*, we note a gesture that reminds us of du Bellay. The Muses do not frequent the salvage soil of Ireland, and the poet describes his rhymes as rude and rustic. But his satire is reserved not for the place of exile but for the English court. In *Colin Clout* he is glad to return to his sheep and his fellow-shepherds. The life is here the simple life, figured forth in that pastoral symbolism so dear to the renascent spirit. If this is anything more than a literary flourish, it means that Ireland was for Spenser a point of detachment, from which with the aid of his friends, his books, and his Muse, he could get the line and level of the moral life. On the other hand, Ireland in the second half of the sixteenth century was not precisely a scene of pastoral peace; so that in *Colin Clout* we look upon two pictures, one of piping shepherds, and one of wailing and wretchedness, bloody issues and leprosies, grisly famine, the nightly bodrags, and the hue and cry. And

---

[1] Compare Chamard, *Joachim Du Bellay, Travaux et Mémoires de l'Université de Lille*, Tome VIII, Lille, 1900.

yet these harsh realities against the background of the Irish scene, when contrasted with Elizabethan court life (that other pole of Spenser's experience), could have given only sharper definition to the dualism of nature and art which was woven closely into the fabric of the poet's thought.

No student of Spenser should overlook the fifteen years that he passed in the midst of danger and romantic scenery. Moreover, the high adventure of the moral life found here its apt illustration and its concrete setting in the efforts of Elizabethan gentlemen to reclaim for God and for their Queen the wild and unregenerate realm of Ireland. Journeying through this land of superstition and witchcraft,[2] Spenser, himself a knight of Gloriana, was, in the heart of deep forests and at every turn of his lonely path, exposed to ambuscade and sudden attack. Here and there in symbolism or in direct description he gives us familiar bits of Irish landscape. He found similitudes for human conflict in the troubled waters of the Irish sound or in contending tides and currents where the Shannon meets the sea. The villains that crowd about the House of Temperance are likened to the gnats that swarm at evening over the fens of Allan. Even more arresting than these passages are those in which the poet describes the scenery about the castle of Kilcolman with attention to the myths of river and mountain. It is the Vale of Arlo that he sketches in greatest detail, shut in by ranges to the north and east, from the peaks of which hurry the mountain streams to feed the rivers of the valley. Here we may suppose one would read his Ariosto and his Benevieni with a difference, and table talk with Bryskett, Fenton, and Raleigh would take a freer range. At any rate it was here that the nymphs once had their residence and that Nature held her court.

Before the Court of Nature in the Vale of Arlo appears Mutability claiming sovereignty alike over gods and men. She argues that everything is subject to change and that she is therefore the true ruler of the universe. Neither the elements—earth, air, fire—nor nature; neither man, the celestial bodies, nor the gods themselves are permanent. This imperfect statement of the Heraclitan flux and flow is corrected by Nature's Platonism. Though all may suffer change, the universe is returning through a fixed and preordained cycle to a fixed and permanent source. As the planets keep to their courses, as spring annually returns in the procession of the months, so the soul passing through all vicissitudes of fortune will at length rest in the bosom of the father whence it came. The confused and troubled action of the Faerie Queene, in which Holiness, Temperance, Chastity, Friendship, Justice, and Courtesy battle in the armor of God against all unrighteousness closes with a note of faith in the Eternal—"in whom there is neither variableness nor shadow of turning":—

---

[2] "At this period there was a general complaint against witchcraft, which even the Earl of Ormond did not blush to assign as the sole cause of the rebellion of his brothers." *State Papers, Ireland*, 1574–1585; Preface, p. 44.

> Then gin I think on that which Nature sayd,
> Of that same time when no more change shall be
> But steadfast rest of all things, firmly stayd
> Upon the pillours of eternity,
> That is contrayr to Mutabilitie;
> For all that moveth doth in change delight:
> But thenceforth all shall rest eternally
> With him that is the God of Sabbaoth hight:
> O that great Sabbaoth God graunt me that Sabaoths sight![3]

It should be clear from what has been said that Ireland for Spenser was in part at least the country in which he had fed his imagination, cultivated his friendships, and nourished his faith; there he had found Nature dwelling among the hills. But Ireland to our poet-philosopher was also the Irish question; and when he turned to this great problem of the centuries I cannot believe that he failed to apply to it a political philosophy consonant with the morality and religion of the *Faerie Queene*. Yet Spenser's contribution to the Irish question has dealt with Ireland and the Irish in a way to inflame the wrath of Celtic and Catholic critics. "Almost every page of the State of Ireland," declares a writer in the *Dublin Review*,[4] "is a violation of the morality of the Fairy Queen." "Spenser," he says, "was prepared by his previous idolatry of absolute power to exhibit in his State of Ireland a spirit which better suits a law of Woden than the day star of English poesy;" and further on, "his (Desmond's) estate was parcelled among English adventurers, and Kilcolman, with three thousand acres, fell to the lot of Spenser. To this circumstance, to the same fell spirit that haunts the usurper on his throne, or the brigand in his cave, we must attribute the sad metamorphosis of the angel of poesy into a dark spirit in politics, gloating over the atrocious

---

[3] The background of Irish Scenery in the *Faerie Queene* and the light that the Mutability cantos throw upon Spenser's understanding of the Irish question are subjects treated suggestively in an unsigned review, "Spenser in Ireland," published in the *Edinburgh Review*, 201 (1905), 164 ff. For the Irish rivers in Spenser's poetry see, further, P. W. Joyce, *Fraser's Magazine*, N. S. Vol. 17, 315 ff., and Keightley, *Notes and Queries*, Series 4, Vol. 4, 169 ff.; compare, too, Keightley, *Fraser's Magazine*, October, 1859. One may consult, too, "Spenser's Irish Residences" by a Dreamer, *Dublin University Magazine* 22 (1843), 538 ff. The article in the *Monitor*, "Edmund Spenser and his Relation to Ireland," I have not seen.

Two passages from the Edinburgh article may here be quoted:—"He [Spenser] could conceive no greater injustice to Ireland, nothing more injurious to the well-being of his adopted country, than the making her the sport of English politicians, or the arena for the rivalries of the English courtiers who contended for the favour of Queen Elizabeth. Inconsistency or inconstancy in action, lack of purpose and vacillation on the part of the representatives of the Crown, he considered injurious alike to both the English and the Irish elements of the population" (p. 185). "The first stanza of Canto VI, with the two stanzas which have alone reached us of the 'unperfite' eighth canto, plainly bespeak the pessimism of the poet in his latter days. Convinced of the ultimate triumph of the principle of constancy in the moral and spiritual world, he yet despairs of witnessing the effective assertion in the actual world in which he moved of the principle of unswerving consistency of purpose and action" (186).

[4] *Dublin Review*, December, 1844 (No. 34): "The Works of Edmund Spenser."

horrors of the Munster war, and sternly urging their perpetration against the Irish in Ulster." "The poison [of the *Veue*] must operate more fatally, coming from a hand from which no evil could be suspected." And referring to the Legend of Sir Artegal in the fifth book of the *Faerie Queene:* "to make him [Lord Grey] the personation of a virtue of which his whole life was a profanation is an outrage unparalleled in the annals of literary curiosities. An ironical hymn to purity in the dens of a brothel, a hymn to pity on the lips of the lurking assassin, or the hymn of the atheists of '92 around the altars of God, might be as bad; but what could be worse?"

To meet such attacks as this the Reverend Alexander B. Grosart brought up his heavy artillery.[5] His purpose is "to vindicate the good name alike of Lord Deputy and Secretary and England against impudent mendacities." "Sir John Pope Hennessy, in his Raleigh in Ireland (1883) and Irishmen generally," declares our gentle divine, "have turned this incident on the very threshold of Lord Grey's government of Ireland to shameless account against the Lord Deputy and Spenser in their passionate resolve to defame our England." However, "before the State Documents the sentimental perversions and artful pathos of Sir John Pope Hennessy will be seen in their true light." The charges against Grey and Spenser Grosart describes as "so heinous and disproved, so damning all around, that it is imperative to meet them as is now done conclusively." Sir John Hennessy's book is "as treacherously skilful as was the kiss of Judas in its pseudo-pathetic vein of condemnation;—a more misleading, lopsided 'History' (save the mark!) has rarely been palmed upon the world." And as for the article in the Dublin Review, it is "a scandalous paper," "pitiably partizan and perpetually blundering."

Into the shouting and tumult of this particular controversy I do not intend to enter. Whether or not Grosart's defense of Grey and Spenser on the ground of military necessity and military precedent will stand the test of dispassionate inquiry, I am not prepared to say. If, however, we would be fair to Spenser, we should remember not only that his "sentiments long rendered his name abhorrent to the native population" of Ireland, but that they arose from an understanding of the significance of the Irish situation. "It is monstrous," Grosart says, "to ignore that it was a death struggle in which England's life was at stake as well as Ireland's, England's Future as well as Ireland's Present." As early as 1570 the Pope had declared English subjects released from loyalty to their Queen;[6] and

[5] *Complete Works of Edmund Spenser,* Vol. 1, p. 136 ff.
[6] The text of the bull may be found in Carl Mirbt's *Quellen zur Geschichte des Papstum und des römischen Katholizismus,* Zweite Auflage, Tübingen und Leipzig, 1901, 266-267 (§338). For the reception of the bull in France, see Strype, *Annals of the Reformation,* II, 17–18. In Lingard, *History of England,* VI, 319, I have noted the following: "In the bull of his [Gregory XIII.'s] predecessor Ireland had not been named: but the omission was now supplied; and Gregory signed, though he did not publish, a new bull, by which Elizabeth was declared to have forfeited the crown of Ireland no less than that of England."

a succession of events preceding and following the Armada revealed the plans of the Jesuits and Philip the Second to bring about the Catholic conquest of England. The back door of England in the sixteenth century swung ajar for the emissaries of continental imperialism. When Spenser wrote the *Veue*, he knew that England had long been swarming with Jesuits, that seminarists from Douay had been attempting to undermine the loyalty of his fellow-countrymen to their Queen, and he had vividly in mind the disclosures of the abortive Throckmorton rebellion, in which even the Spanish minister had been involved. The massacre of the garrison at Smerwick, for which Lord Grey's critics particularly censure him, was dictated by the circumstance that the garrison harbored a large number of Spanish soldiers.[7] "Every port and town and upland town," Sir John Dowdall writes to Lord Burghley, "is furnished with superstitious priests. The townsmen and merchants do transport them from Spain to Ireland, and so from Ireland to Spain again, and

[7] *Cambridge Modern History*, III, 287 ff. Innes, *England under the Tudors*, p. 321, says "Grey doubtless regarded the measures as a just return for the doings of the Inquisition' and the punishment of English sailors as pirates, for his retort to the garrison's overtures had been that their presence in England was piracy. But the whole business illustrates the sheer ruthlessness which characterized both sides, at least when there was a technical excuse for denying belligerents' rights to the vanquished." See, further, article 571, *State Papers, Foreign*, 1577–1578, 423 ff.: *Designs Against England:* "There has been proposed to the Most Christian King on the part of certain Italians favouring the Church of Rome, a conspiracy with a view to exterminate all the reformed Churches of Christendom and utterly destroy all princes and others who profess the Gospel as well according to the French as the Augustan confession, by means of intelligence between the Kings of Spain and France and the Pope, with other princes whom they call Catholic.

"First, they point out that the reformed Churches were first founded in Germany, having been courageously protected by some of the princes of that country, among others the Electors Palatine and of Saxony, who still uphold them, and that the sovereigns of England notably the present Queen, with the view of securing their own realms, foster, to the injury especially of the Kings of France and Spain, the heresies which are always troubling their realms, and now promise a great revolt throughout the Low Countries, and consequently in the rest of their dominions. In order therefore to cut away these troubles at the root, to stop the favour shown to the heretics, and cut off their resources, and to bring all Christendom back under the Pope's authority, it is necessary to fall upon their chief supporters, and especially on the Queen of England.

"Don John has been designated to the chief command in the execution of this enterprise, as the most suitable person they could find; having all the qualities required for a great captain to bring the matter to a happy issue, being young, prudent, valiant and experienced.

"His past good fortune, the disposition of affairs in the Low Countries, the notion that he might marry the Queen of Scots through the practice of the House of Guise, the assurance that he would be accompanied by many persons in his confidence, who living on the fruits of war try all means of continuing it, stimulate him to the undertaking."—John is to receive material support from the King of Spain, the Pope, and the King of Sweden.

"The manner of execution will be to take these forces to Ireland, and there break into [entamer] the English State. They claim to have intelligence with a good number of English, Scottish, and other Catholics who have fled thither; and these after the first battle, in the event of victory being on the side of Don John, promise to declare themselves, to get a footing

likewise to France, which swarm up and down the whole country seducing the people and the best sorts to draw them from God and their allegiance to the Prince. Every town is established with sundry schools where the noblemen and gentlemen's sons of the country do repair; these schools have a superstitious or an idolatrous schoolmaster, and each school is overseen by a Jesuit, whereby the youth of the whole kingdom are corrupted and poisoned with more superstition and disobedience than all the rest of the Popish crew in all Europe."[8] A communication like this, which might be easily paralleled from the *Calendar of Irish Papers*, gives to our picture a touch of Prussian blue. If we now fill in a few more details, the seriousness of the situation will sufficiently appear. From the *Calendar* I take the following:—"Turlagh Lynagh assisted by the Scottish King's forces and they of Munster and Connaught by the supply of Spaniards to be landed at Sligo, should break out all at once. Turlough looking for aid from Scotland and Spain expected to be made King of Ireland. He said that the realm was carelessly left without force and no man of war to govern it, and therefore they thought it best not to lose so good an occasion, especially when they were offered so great aid from foreign parts."[9] And it was about this time that Pope Gregory XIII. was "amusing himself with the dream of making his son, Signor Jacomo, King of Ireland."[10]

Whether or not, then, we champion Lord Grey's harsh measures in Ireland and our English poet's defense of them, we should try to see the

---

on the main land, to raise their party, and favour the landing of 8,000 or 10,000 men, who will be sent."—The rest of the entry is worth reading.

Compare Holinshed VI:436:—"It was thoroughlie concluded between the Pope and King Philip, to make a thorough conquest of all Ireland; and so consequentlie as time should serve, to doo the like with England;" and in regard to the surrender of Smerwick, *ibid.*, VI: 437–438:—"But before anie assault given, he first summoned the fort; requiring of them who they were, what they had there to doo, by whom they were sent, and whie they fortified in hir majesties land, and required therewith to yield up the fort. But they answered that they were sent some from the holie father, which had given that realme to king Philip; and some from king Philip, who was to receive and recover that land to the holie Church of Rome, which by hir maiesties means was become schismaticall, and out of the Church, with other reprochfull speeches; and that therfore they were in that respect to keepe what they had and to recover what they had not." Strype, *Annals* II, 630 ff., says in regard to the seminarists at Douay:— "The Pope gave them an annual Pension, or rather a maintenance: purposely to plot and contrive ways to expel the Queen, and demolish the Church of *England*. After they had tarried there some years, upon some troubles they removed most of them to *Scotland*. Where the Queen of *Scots* allowed them a Pension, and liberty to set up another School for the education of *English* Youth, who would come thither. Here they were taught all manner of ways to divide the Protestants of *England*, in Principles of Religion, as also to withdraw them from the Form of Prayer established."

[8] *State Papers, Ireland*, (1592–1596), p. 487.

[9] *State Papers, Ireland*, 1574–1585, article 39, p. 520; compare in the same volume article 43, p. 521.

[10] *State Papers, Ireland*, 1574–1585, Preface, p. 43.

Irish Question in its true colors; we should remember that Ireland in the lifetime of Spenser was a bridgehead of Spanish imperialism. We should also—and this is my special task—examine the *Veue* and the fifth book of the *Faerie Queene* to ascertain whether our poet rested his case on any surer foundation than that of military necessity and military precedent. I contend that such an examination will reveal Spenser neither as the dual personality envisaged by the Dublin Review nor, according to Professor Greenlaw,[11] as the interpreter of the Machiavellian politic rightly understood, but as the "sage and serious" poet looking to his central philosophy of life as his final justification. Indeed the *Veue* when brought into relation with the fifth book of the *Faerie Queene* (and the two should always be studied together) appears as a quite intelligible application of Spenser's moral philosophy. One of the questions which the Irish wars raised in the shrewd mind of Elizabeth they raised also in the philosophical mind of Spenser, as a moment's comparison of the *Veue* with the *Calendar of Irish Papers* will make clear. In defending Lord Grey, who by his severity had incurred the displeasure of his Queen, Spenser is trying to meet Elizabeth on common ground. What this common ground is, what is the fundamental philosophy of Spenser's apology, how that philosophy connects with the philosophy of the *Faerie Queene*, and from what contemporary quarter it drew its inspiration, I will now attempt to show.

The Dictionary of National Biography[12] is right in some measure when it says that "Spenser wrote of Ireland altogether from the point of view of the Elizabethan Englishman. He allowed no recognition of Irish claims and rights. English laws were to be enforced and Irish nationality to be uprooted by the sword." The question was indeed not one of Irish rights as distinct from and opposed to English rights, but of the extent to which the enforcement of English rights and English laws should be instructed and directed by political and humanitarian considerations. Of these considerations, Elizabeth in her dispatches makes a good deal. In the instructions which Lord Grey took to Ireland he was told to "have an especial care that by the oppression and insolencies of the soldiers our good subjects may not be alienated from us;"[13] and Grey is particularly cautioned against being too strict in religious matters.[14] Indeed there were many complaints that the Queen's attempts to season justice with mercy were ill-timed and that they embarrassed the direction of the English campaigns. Sentleger laments her ill-considered tolerance;[15] and Sir John Dowdall, writing to Lord Burghley under date of March

---

[11] *Modern Philology*, VII, 187 ff. See below p. 64 ff.
[12] Article *Spenser*.
[13] *Carew Papers*, July 15, 1580 (No. 422).
[14] *State Papers, Ireland*, 1574–1585, p. 275.
[15] *State Papers, Ireland*, 1574–1585; Preface, p. 100.

9 (1595–1596),[16] exclaims: "Who is it of them but hath felt of Her Majesty's mercy and a great many that have been rewarded by her bounty for small deserts or none, if they be governed by a mild hand and accounted of, and so rewarded, they swell so in pride and say that the Governor standeth in doubt or feareth them, but if he be severe with justice in one hand and the sword in the other to use it according to equity, they say he is a tyrant, and desire to have such a one removed, being most meet to govern this nation." In a similar strain Waterhouse had written to Walsyngham (December 23, 1580)[17]: "If the Queen will use mildness with the traitors, she would do better to discharge her army at once." On the other hand, White, the Master of the Rolls, approves her course. He writes to Burghley,[18] May 25, 1582: "Her Majesty's clement and merciful disposition towards her people is the greatest comfort that ever came into this land, Elizabeth, the Amor Hiberniae above all the Princes that ever reigned."

Now Grey's apologists were concerned to redeem his character in general as well as his Irish policy in particular. He is represented in the *Calendar of State Papers*[19] as well as in the *Veue* as a man of merciful disposition, upon whom a stern task had been imposed. Those who know Grey, Irenaeus of the dialogue says, "knewe him to be most gentell, affable, loving, and temperate; but that the necessitye of that present state of thinges enforced him to that violence, and almost changed his very naturall disposition. But otherwise he was so farr from delighting in bloud, that oftentimes he suffered not just vengeance to fall where it was deserved: and even some of those which were afterwardes his accusers had tasted to much of his mercye, and were from the gallowes brought to be his accusers."[20] This, with other passages which might be cited, accepts Elizabeth's premise that justice in Ireland should be seasoned with mercy, but opposes the conclusion that Lord Grey had fallen short of this standard. Furthermore, the passages in the *Legend of Justice* devoted to equity and

[16] *State Papers, Ireland*, 1574–1585, March 9, 1595–1596. Compare "A Declaration by the Lord Deputy and Council" (*State Papers*, 1596, No. 261): "The way to suppress the Northern rebels is to prosecute them with a sharp war, and thereby extirpate those who are obstinate."

[17] *State Papers, Ireland*, 1574–1585, p. 276; *ibid.*, p. 274: The Queen writes to Grey expressing the wish that "those who have been spared had been reserved for her to have extended either justice or mercy;" *ibid.*, p. 299, Privy Council to Grey: In reply to a request for an additional 1000 men "to war against Turlough Lynagh," suggests "an offer of pardon and confirmation of certain things to be offered to Turlough Lynagh;" *ibid.*, p. 299: "Proclamation set forth by the Queen in England, offering her gracious pardon generally, with one exception of the Earl of Desmond, etc." Compare the reply of Grey, *ibid.*, p. 300.

[18] *State Papers*, 1574–1585, p. 369.

[19] "Grey has never taken the life of any, however evil, that submitted;" *State Papers, Ireland*, 1574–1585, p. 301. In his letter to the Queen regarding the Smerwick Massacre Grey wrote: "a hard and forcible hand I too well find must bring them [the Irish] to duty, which I confess falls not with my nature;" *State Papers, Ireland*, 1574–1585, Preface, p. 74.

[20] *Globe Spenser*, p. 655.

mercy—the episodes of Isis Church and the House of Mercilla—in which Spenser declares the loyalty and love which the Lord Deputy felt for the Queen, at once merciful and militant, and those other passages in which he is represented as recalling Talus from the stern execution of justice,— all of these show that Spenser was defending Lord Grey as one who in the practice of justice was loyal to the principle of clemency.[21]

More particularly, Spenser undertook to defend Lord Grey against the suspicion of intolerant Protestantism. There seems to be sufficient evidence for his religious zeal. His speech in defense of William Davison, the Queen's secretary, is described by Camden[22] as inflamed with religious ardor; and Elizabeth felt that his anti-Catholic feelings would carry him to extremes in the Irish campaigns. He himself complains under date of December 22, 1580, that his obedience to the Queen's "warning against being strict in religious matters is very harmful."[23] To meet the criticism of religious intolerance stated or implied, Spenser in the *Veue* declares that it was Grey's belief that "instruction in religion needeth quiett times, and ere we seeke to settle a sounde discipline in the clargye we must purchase peace unto the layetye;"[24] and that "in planting of religion thus much is needfull to be observed, that it be not sought forcebly to be impressed into them with terrour and sharpe penalties, as nowe is the manner, but rather delivered and intimated with mildeness and gentleness soe as it may not be hated before it be understood."[25]

The fundamental issue, then, raised by Lord Grey's administration of his deputyship concerns the relation in the abstract between justice and tolerance; and the issue is considered in general and more particularly in its religious aspects. In discussing this issue I will turn not to the familiar classical sources of Spenser's ethical system, but to contemporary speculation under classical and other influences which was presumably congenial to a low churchman from Pembroke College, Cambridge, who had satirized Bishop Aylmer, praised Archbishop Grindal, and enjoyed the patronage of Leicester.

[21] See below p. 53 ff. Holinshed (VI:450) describes Grey as follows: "The said Lord Greie was a man of great nobilitie, and of as honourable and ancient descent, one that feareth God in true religion, and dutifull in hir majestie in all obedience. And albeit he had deserved well of that Irish nation, and had sowed the good seeds of notable services, as well for his martiall services, as for his civill government; yet he reped (as his predecessors before him) but darnell and cockle."
[22] *Dictionary of National Biography*, article *Grey*.
[23] *State Papers, Ireland*, 1574–1588, p. 275.
[24] *Globe Spenser*, p. 646.
[25] *Op. cit.*, p. 679.

CHAPTER II

The Cult of Nationalism and Tolerance in England and France

In the period of the Reformation and the Religious Wars the culture of the Renascence was endangered by fanaticism. Passionate and vindictive loyalties delayed the triumph of liberal thought. The excesses of religious enthusiasm insulted that ideal of the tempered passions and the open mind which it was the concern of the humanist to inculcate; and as an instrument of reform the pliant Erasmian disposition, open to impressions, barbed with irony, impatient of the mechanism of dogma, gave way before the inquisition and the *auto-da-fé*. Everywhere, according to Janet, Protestant intolerance imitated and equaled the intolerance of Catholics. Beza, Calvin, and even Melanchthon argued strongly for the punishment of Catholics.[26] In Spenser's time the strategic answer to the Catholic challenge was made not so much by those who like Beza adopted Catholic tactics as by moderates of both religions who recognized in the spirit of religious tolerance the salvation of the state.

The outstanding documents of Anglican religious literature are apologetic. To meet the attacks of both Catholics and Puritans the chief apologists of the Establishment, Jewel and Hooker, interpreted the English Reformation as a revival on the one hand of early Christianity and patristic Catholicism, as contrasted with the scholastic and corrupt Catholicism of the Romanists; on the other hand, as a conservative bulwark protecting at once the state and the traditional church against the extravagance and the vagaries of the extreme Protestant sects. In his *Apologia Ecclesiae Anglicanae*,[27] Bishop Jewel compares the Romanists with the Anabaptists and the Libertines in that they all shake off the yoke of civil power.[28] An exponent of order and a champion of an uncontaminated Catholic tradition, he regarded the Pope as a Lord of Misrule and the extremists among the Puritans as irresponsible and licentious. He comes out frankly as a defender of the sovereignty of the Prince in the political sphere and of the Bible and reason in the sphere of religion. "As for us," he writes,[29] "we run not for succour to the fire, as these men's guise is; but we run to the Scriptures; neither do we reason with the sword but with the word of God; and therewith as saith Tertullian, 'we do feed our faith; by it do we stir up our hope, and strengthen our confidence.'" And again:[30] "And

---

[26] Janet, *Histoire de la Science Politique, Troisième Édition;* II, p. 15.
[27] *The Works of John Jewell*, Part III, Parker Society, Cambridge, 1848.
[28] *Op. cit.*, p. 75.
[29] *Op. cit.*, p. 84.
[30] *Op. cit.*, pp. 85–86.

as for their religion, if it be of so long continuance as they would have men ween it is, why do they not prove it so by the examples of the primitive church, and by the fathers and councils of old time? Why lieth so ancient a cause thus long in the dust destitute of an advocate? Fire and sword they have had always ready at hand; but as for the old councils and the fathers, all mum not a word. They did surely against all reason to begin first with these bloody and extreme means, if they could have found other more easy and gentle ways."

The line of argument adopted by Jewel in the *Apologia* was followed out elaborately by his more celebrated disciple, the author of the *Ecclesiastical Polity*. Like Jewel, Hooker[31] argues for a renascence of early Christianity, and like him he contends against the revolutionary teachings of the extreme Puritans. The greater part of his book is occupied with a defense of the Anglican organization and administration of ecclesiastical affairs. But his distinguished performance contains a discussion of topics far more fundamental than the ordination and authority of bishops and the reason of ritual. Students of jurisprudence turn to him for an admirable diagram of laws eternal, human, natural, and divine; and for a doctrine of sovereignty that is closely related to his philosophy of law. His book is notable throughout for its tolerant spirit. "My meaning," he declared, "is not to provoke any but rather to satisfy all tender consciences." "His Ecclesiastical Polity," writes Professor Usher,[32] "was the preparation of the English church settlement to unite all men under one common banner, to satisfy all tender consciences, so that none might be excluded from that great church of the Living Christ which he would found upon the law of Nature and the Reason of Man." He is concerned, indeed, not only to defend the divine source and responsibility of the kingship but the eternal reason that lies behind and beneath the law of God and all laws derivative from it. On this account, Hooker is rightly regarded not only as the chief apologist of the Anglican Establishment but as an unconscious forerunner of such a rationalized defense of monarchical institutions as Hobbes expounded in the following century.[33]

Unfortunately the temper of all Anglicans was not that of Jewel and Hooker. Although Whitgift[34] naturally approved the reasoned defense of the Church in the *Ecclesiastical Polity*, he can not be said to have administered his high office in the spirit of "our meek and gentle Mr. Hooker." His strict enforcement of the *Statute of Uniformity* not only stirred up the hornet's nest of Martin Marprelate but called forth the censure of Bacon and even of Burghley.[35] And yet this austere executive showed himself

---

[31] For the relation of Hooker to Bancroft, see Usher, *Reconstruction of the English Church*, I, 72 ff.
[32] *Op. cit.*, I, 77.
[33] *Cambridge Modern History*, III, 348.
[34] *Cambridge Modern History*, III, 347.
[35] *Cambridge Modern History*, III, 342.

liberal in matters of doctrine. That his austerity was addressed not so much to the dogma of the Church as to its law and order, appears in the celebrated *Lambeth Articles*, which were rejected by the Queen. When we compare him with Jewel, Hooker, and Grindal, we recognize that the contrast is not in narrowness of mind but in harshness of temper.

Whitgift did not, however, differ from his fellow-churchmen in his devotion to the ideal of sovereignty. In the spirit of Bodin's Harmonic Justice, he applied the autocratic principle to the polity, the democratic principle to the doctrine of the Church. His persecutions—if we call them that—were political rather than religious. And in general under the Anglican Establishment there were no martyrs, as has often been remarked, but only traitors.[36]

If this applies to the dissenting Protestants, it is applicable *a fortiori* to a large if not the entire body of English Catholics. Compared to the Catholic menace the opposition of the Puritans carried comparatively little danger except such as might arise from the weakening effect of internal dissension. Men like Leicester and Sidney combined with their loyalty to the Queen an interest in European Protestantism and a sympathy with English Puritans. Coming in part through the intermediary of Sidney under the influence of the leading Protestant thinkers of the time, the circle of Spenser naturally viewed Protestantism in its large philosophical and international aspects. Like our modern democracy it was a bond of freedom which united England with the Netherlands and the Protestant princes of Germany against the imperial Catholicism of Philip II. With their outlook upon the religious problems of their day Spenser and his friends doubtless considered the differences of English Protestants as insignificant when compared with the very serious Catholic peril.

[36] Professor Usher, *op. cit.*, I, 40 f., writes: "Every attempt to alter the religious settlement became a blow at the State; every refusal to attend Church or to accept the ordinances of the Establishment, savoured of treason to the Crown; and, in turn, whatever affected the stability and strength of the State, inevitably reacted upon the Church. When adhesion to the ecclesiastical system was made a test of political loyalty, the good of the Church, as an institution, was naturally subordinated to the safety of the State. For years, every ecclesiastical problem had been regarded in fact not as a religious but as a political issue, to be handled circumspectly and cautiously, for in its train might follow ruin for Church and State alike." Compare Innes, *England Under the Tudors*, 417 ff.:—"In writing of the persecutions under Elizabeth alike of Catholics and of Puritans, it is not uncommon to imply that the political argument in their defence was a mere pretext with a theological motive. As a matter of fact, however, the distinction between Elizabeth's and Mary's persecutions is a real one. Broadly speaking, it is now the universally received view that no man ought to be penalized on the score of opinions conscientiously held, however erroneous they may be; but that if those opinions find expression in anti-social acts, the acts must be punished. Punishment of opinions is rightly branded as persecution. Now although in effect not a few persons, Puritans or Catholics, were put to death by Elizabeth, and many more imprisoned or fined—as they would have said themselves for conscience' sake—this was the distinction specifically recognized by her; which without justifying her persecutions, differentiates them from those of her predecessors."

The spirit of religious tolerance which was characteristic of the political and international Protestantism of Spenser's circle took an even wider range in the philosophical mind of Bacon. With the recognition that indiscriminate anti-Catholicism was unjust to many loyal English Catholics,[37] the essentially political issue was more and more sharply defined, and religious toleration as such had a larger opportunity. In their efforts to make religious tolerance serve the ends of national integrity and security, men like Bacon were squarely in line with a party in France which undertook to subordinate sectarianism to nationalism. This cult of nationalism, the sober Protestant and Catholic thinkers of the time—however Machiavellian might have been the politicians—undertook to defend on broad philosophical grounds, and in some ideal way to bring into accord with the principle of religious tolerance the doctrine of political sovereignty.

Bacon, who thought that a kingdom was a model of heaven and that "reverence is that wherewith princes are girt from God,"[38] spoke clearly and strongly for tolerance in his *Advertisement Touching the Controversies of the Church of England* (1589).[39] He declared that the then state of religion needed not so much "the general canon and sentence of Christ against heretics," as "the admonition of St. James, 'Let every man be swift to hear, slow to speak, slow to wrath;' and that the wound is no way dangerous, except we poison it with our remedies;—if any shall be offended at this voice, *Vos estis fratres*; ye are brethren, why strive ye? he shall give a

---

[37] The case of conscientious English Catholics who were loyal to their country and Queen is stated with force and apparent sincerity in a letter from Mr. George More, "perhaps of the family of Sir Thomas More," reprinted in Strype's *Whitgift*, IV, 505 ff. (*anno* 1597): "Would to God therefore," he says in the course of the letter, "it might please her Majesty to grant Toleration of Religion: wherby mens minds might be appeased, and joyned, all in one, for the Defence of our Country. We see what Safety it hath been for France. . . . Wel may Mens Bodies be forced, but not their minds. And where Force is used, Love is lost. And there the Prince and State is in Danger." Strype's comment upon the letter is to the point:—"The State of the *English Romanists* at this Time was the worse, by Reason of the King of *Spain's* implacable Malice against *England*, and his fierce Purpose of invading the Realm, and destroying the Queen, being set on by many *English* Priests and *Jesuits* abroad; particularly *Holt* and *Parsons*. Who had a great Stroke with that King, and were continually exciting him to those Courses. And it fared the worse with al the Queen's Subjects of that Religion, both at home as wel as abroad, for the malicious minds of some." The disposition in favor of religious tolerance expressed by men like Hooker and Bacon appears to have been shared generally by the people. I have found in Innes, *op. cit.*, 290 f. what has impressed me as a judicious description of the situation:—"The bulk of the population was quite content with conformity to a compromise, and was tolerant of a very considerable theoretical disagreement, and even of actual nonconformity, so long as it was not actively aggressive. It was not till Jesuits on one side, and ultra-puritanism on the other, developed an active propaganda directed against the established order that there was any general desire to strike hard at either; nor did even the puritan parliaments display any violent anti-Catholic animus till roused by the insult to the nation of the Bull of Deposition."

[38] Spedding, *Life*, V, 145.

[39] *Op. cit.*, VIII, 74 ff.

great presumption against himself, that he is the party that doth his brother wrong." "The controversies," he holds, "be not of the highest nature;" for it is not now as it was of old when the Catholics were compelled to follow the heretics "with all subtility of decisions and determinations" and when "it was an ingenious and subtle matter to be a Christian." "Therefore seeing the accidents are they that breed the peril, and not the things themselves in their own nature, it is meet the remedies be applied unto them, by opening what it is on either part, that keepeth the wound green." He protests against "this immodest and deformed manner of writing lately entertained, whereby matters of religion are handeled in the style of the stage."—"To turn religion into a comedy or satire; to search and rip up wounds with a laughing countenance; to intermix Scripture and scurrility sometime in one sentence; is a thing far from the devout reverence of a Christian, and scant beseeming the honest regard of a sober man." A fool is to be answered, "but not by becoming like unto him."

Having paid his respects in this manner to the more noisy and intolerant controversialists, Bacon proceeds to inquire into the accidents and circumstances of the controversies. I will not take space to reproduce the capital topics of his discourse, but I will cull from the text a few quotations to show the spirit and direction of his thought. To those who "infer the solicitation for the peace of the Church to proceed from carnal sense," he replies in the words of St. Paul: "Whilst there is amongst you zeal and contention are ye not carnal?" He beseeches the Lord to multiply his blessings and graces upon other churches: "God grant that we may contend with other churches, as the vine with the olive, which of us beareth best fruit; and not as the brier with the thistle, which of us is most unprofitable." "I pray God to inspire the bishops with a fervent love and care of the people; and that they may not so much urge things in controversy, as things out of controversy, which all men confess to be gracious and good." "I dislike that laws be contemned, or disturbers be unpunished. But laws are likened to the grape, that being too much pressed yield an hard and unwholesome wine." Speaking of still another group, of those that affect "certain cognizances and differences," although they have not cut themselves off from the body of the church, Bacon declares: "Yea, be a man endued with great virtues and fruitful in good works, yet if he concur not with them, they term him (in derogation) a civil and moral man, and compare him to Socrates or some heathen philosopher: whereas the wisdom of Scriptures teacheth us contrariwise to judge and denominate men religious according to their works of the second table; because they of the first are often counterfeited and practised in hypocrisy. So, St. John saith that a man doth vainly boast of loving God whom he hath not seen, if he love not his brother whom he hath seen." "And as they censure virtuous men by the names of civil and moral, so do they censure men truly and godly wise (who see into the vanity of their assertions) by the name of politiques;

saying that their wisdom is but carnal and savoring of man's brain." "The word (the bread of life) they toss up and down, they break it not." "They forget that there are sins on the right hand, as well as on the left; and that the word is double-edged, and cutteth on both sides, as well the superstitious observances as the profane transgressions."

With the views of Bacon might be compared those which Harvey has set forth in *Pierces Supererogation*.[40] This friend of Spenser's here asks what could grow out of the controversy "but to make every man mad-brayned, and desperate; but a general contempt of all good order, in Saying or Dooing; but an Universal Topsy-turvy?—Had it not beene a better course, to have followed Aristotles doctrine: and to have confuted levity with gravity, vanity with discretion, rashness with advise, madnesse with sobriety, fier with water, ridiculous Martin with reverend Cooper?—I am not to dispute as a professed Devine; or to determine, as a severe Censour: but a scholler may deliver his opinion with reason.—It is neither the Excess, nor the Defect, but the Meane, that edifyeth.—Superstition, and Credulitie, are simple Creatures: but what are Contempt, and tumult?" Employing here the argument of the policists, he declares: "The difference of Commonwealthes, or regiments, requireth a difference of lawes, and orders: and those lawes, and orders, are most soverain, that are most agreeable to the regiment, and best proportioned to the Commonwealth.—Howbeit none so fitt to reconcile contradictions, or to accord differences, as he that distinguisheth Times, Places, Occasions, and other swaying Circumstances; high pointes in governement, either Civill, or Ecclesisticall.—In cases indifferent, or arbitrary, what so equall in generall, as Indifferency: or so requisite in speciall, as conformity to the positive Lawe, to the custome of the Countrey, or the present occasion? To be perverse, and obstinate without necessary cause, is a peevish folly: when by such a duetyfull, and justifiable order of proceeding, as by a sacred league, so infinite Variances, and contentions may be compounded.—Were none more scrupulous, then St. Paul, how easily, and gratiously might divers Confutations bee reconciled, that now rage, like Civill Warres? The chiefest matter in question, is no article of beliefe, but a point of pollicy, or governement: wherin a Judiciall Equity being duely observed, what letteth but the particular Lawes, Ordinances, Injunctions, and whole manner of Jurisdiction, may rest in the disposition of Soveraine Autoritie? Whose immediate, or mediate actes, are to be reverenced with Obedience, not countermaunded with sedition, or controled with contention. He is a bold subject, that attempteth to binde the handes of sacred Majesty: and they love controversies well, I trow, that call their Princes proceedinges into Controversie." It will be seen from this passage, which it has seemed worth while to quote at length, that Spenser's scholarly friend, like Bacon,

---

[40] *Works*, Ed. Grosart, II. The quotations that follow will be found at page 131 ff.

Jewel, Hooker, and the French policists, acknowledges his loyalty to the twin ideals of religious tolerance and political sovereignty.

The year in which Bacon's Advertisement was written, 1589, saw a significant change in the alignment of religious and political parties across the channel. Henry III., having weakly temporized with the sinister Spanish party, sought to extricate himself by the murder of the powerful Duke of Guise. This was no sooner done than he realized that his only safety from the outraged Catholics lay in an alliance with the King of Navarre.[41] The consummation of this truce was not only hailed with delight by the war-worn French but was welcomed by the English as furnishing an opportunity for a closer union with France against the common enemy. Burghley wrote on the twenty-seventh of May:—"The world is marvellously changed, when we true Englishmen have cause, for our own quietness, to wish good success to a French king and a king of Scots; and yet they both differ one from another in profession of religion; but seeing that they are enemies of our enemies we have come to join with them in these actions against our enemies."[42] When in the following August Henry III. was himself assassinated and the King of Navarre came to the throne as Henry IV., there was evidently a desire in England to make the *entente cordiale* as cordial as possible. Particularly Elizabeth desired to make it clear that her religion was in line with that of the new king of France, if we can judge from a letter dispatched by Walsingham, Elizabeth's Secretary of State, to Monsieur Critoy, Secretary of France.[43] This interesting document Spedding has no doubt was composed by Bacon. Stressing throughout the point that the crimes for which the English Non-Conformists were punished were crimes against the sovereignty of the Queen and not against the doctrine of the Church, the letter is digested into two principles upon which her Majesty's proceedings have been governed—

I. The one, that consciences are not to be forced, but to be won and reduced by the force of truth, with the aid of time and the use of all good means of instruction and persuasion.

II. The other, that the causes of conscience, when they exceed their bounds and grow to be a matter of faction, lose their nature; and that sovereign princes ought distinctly to punish the practice or (*sic*) contempt, though colored with the pretence of conscience and religion.

When in 1593 Henry entered the Romanist communion, there was no little surprise and chagrin in England; but by 1596—the year in which the *Veue* was written and the last three books of the *Faerie Queene* were published—England and France had come to terms in a defensive and offensive alliance.

Our understanding of Anglo-French relations in the last two decades of the sixteenth century is furthered by comparing the temper of Elizabeth

---

[41] *Cambridge Modern History*, III, 511.
[42] Spedding, *op. cit.*, VIII, 95.
[43] *Ibid.*, 97 ff.

and Henry IV. in matters of religion. In his noble address to the three estates of the realm on the fourth of March, 1589,[44] Henry declared that his policy was one of clemency and peace:—"Although more than any other I regret to see religious differences, and though more than any other I desire to remedy such a situation, nevertheless in full recognition of the truth that it is God alone and not arms and violence that must attend to these matters, I swear before him, engaging faith and honour, the integrity of which I have so far by his grace preserved,—I swear that just as I should not have suffered one to constrain me in matters of conscience, so I shall never allow nor sanction that Catholics should be constrained in theirs, nor in the free exercise of their religion." Further on he avows that he has "long since learned that the true and only means of reuniting people to the service of God and of establishing piety in a state, is gentleness, peace, and true examples, not war and disorders by which wickedness and disorders are born in the world."

But the clemency of Henry of Navarre, like the clemency of Elizabeth, his associate in the Protestant cause, was adjudged by other anti-leaguers but little likely to further the patriotic interests that he had at heart. An effective expression of this point of view is found in the *Satyre Ménippée*.[45]

The *Satyre* consists of a fancied report by a Florentine gentleman of a session of the estates at Paris, to be sent his lord, the Duke of Florence, that the latter might know how admirable was the condition of affairs in the French capital. But it happened that while this gentleman was returning by way of Amiens the driver of his palfrey took French leave of his master, who he had observed was not a good Catholic. The servant, in order to relieve his lord of the necessity of feeding two horses, makes off with one, taking with him besides the satchel in which was contained the manuscript of the *Satyre*. The thief before he had gone very far was arrested; and the manuscript, discovered and translated, in time sees the light of day.

It is not my purpose to dwell at length on the *Satyre Ménippée*; but I would emphasize its importance for an understanding of the politico-religious situation in France, seeking to promote as it does law and order, preaching tolerance, but arraigning sharply Catholic intrigue and violence. It recognizes severity as a necessary means to the establishment of the ideal of the tolerant state; and it contends that mere easy-going tolerance

---

[44] *Recueil des Lettres Missives de Henry IV*, Tome II (1585–1589), 443 ff., in *Collection de Documents Inédits sur l'Histoire de France, Première Série, Histoire Politique*.

[45] *Satyre Ménippée, Kritisch revidierter Text, mit Einleitung und erklärenden Anmerkungen*, von Josef Frank, Oppeln, 1884. An English translation of the *Satyre* was licensed September 28, 1594 and appeared the following year under the title "A Pleasant Satyre or Poesie. Wherein is discovered the Catholicon of Spayne, and the chiefe leaders of the League finelie fetcht over and leide open in their colours." Sidney Lee, who calls attention to the English translation, says that the *Satyre* "helped to guide public opinion in England;" *French Renaissance in England*, p. 298.

such as at times seemed to be the temper of Henry and Elizabeth might prove fatal. In the harangue of Monsieur d'Aubray "pour le tiers-Estat," in which occurs the justly celebrated apostrophe—"O Paris, qui n'es plus Paris, mais spelunque de bestes farouches"—Monsieur d'Aubray asks:— "What laws, what articles, what gospel teaches us to dispossess men of their goods, and kings of their kingdoms, for differences of religion?" On the other hand, kings must guard against an excess of clemency. Then follows a passage which I will summarize in some detail describing the nature of clemency and defining its sphere.

Monsieur d'Aubray declares that though he does not endorse much of the adverse criticism of Henry of Navarre, he recognizes in the Prince one fault,—one, indeed, through which he and others have been much bound to him. Navarre treats us, he says, too gently and indulges us too much. Clemency, which the prince shows in excess, is a virtue highly praiseworthy and one which bears great and long-lasting fruit, however slow it may be in coming. But it is a virtue to be used only by the victorious and those who have no one to resist them. Some attribute it to cowardice and timidity rather than to valor and generosity; for it appears that those that spare their enemies wish that their enemies should do the like to them; or they are afraid that should they show severity, they may be unable to get the better of enemies that are still to be conquered. Other people say that clemency is wholly an imbecility of the heart, judging that he who does not avail himself of his rights is not fully assured of conquering and fears in some way to be conquered. But the philosophers, who have fully treated this matter, have not accounted it a virtue on the part of those who, planning to found a state, have shown themselves gracious and courteous at the outstart of their performances. One may cite, for example, the gentleness that Caesar showed towards the Roman citizens and men-at-arms before he was victorious. That was not clemency but flattery and ambitious courtesy, through which Caesar wished to make himself agreeable to the people and attract everyone to his party. According to the saying of the great *maître d'Estat*: *Imperium occupantibus est clementiae fama*. On the other hand, it was clemency itself which he showed when having conquered Pompey and defeated everyone who could oppose him, he came to Rome without a triumph and pardoned all his capital enemies, restoring them all their goods, their honors, and their dignities. From his conduct, however, much evil came to him, for the very persons whom he had pardoned and to whom he had shown the greatest favor were those who betrayed him and miserably massacred him. There is then a difference between clemency and gentleness (*douceur*). Gentleness belongs ordinarily to women and men of little courage (*la douceur tompe ordinairement aux femmes et aux hommes de petit courage*); but clemency is only in him who does good when he has the power to do what is wholly evil. Our king should defer to employ clemency until he has us all in his power. Furthermore, it is the reverse of clemency, that is cruelty, as Cicero says, to pardon those who deserve to die. Never will civil wars end if we continue to be gracious where severe justice is necessary. The malice of rebels is puffed up and hardened by the gentleness one shows them, because they think that one does not dare to irritate them nor to give them an incentive to do worse than they have done. I make no doubt, that had the king sharply punished all that have fallen in his hands since our troubles began, we should all now be his obedient subjects. But since it has pleased God to make his nature so gentle, gracious, and kindly, we hope still more from him when he shall see us prostrated at his feet, offering him our lives and our goods and asking him pardon for our past faults, inasmuch as now that we are armed to resist and to assail him he lets us have our lives and all that we ask of him.

Keeping in mind, then, the political relations between France and England during the last two decades of the sixteenth century, and with respect to the religious differences of the time, the similarity of Elizabeth's mediatory position to that of Henry of Navarre, we may properly turn to a group of French publicists who deal with the concepts of Justice, Clemency, and Sovereignty in a spirit congenial with that of Hooker, Jewel, and Gabriel Harvey. I refer to the representatives in literature of *les politiques*, a party which opposing extremists among Protestants and Catholics alike, sought in tolerance and peace the salvation of France. Of this cult of sovereignty and tolerance in its speculative aspects I will take as representative three of its distinguished exponents: Michel de l'Hôpital, François de la Noue, and Jean Bodin. Although the policists as a group were reproached with Machiavellian duplicity,[46] these writers sought an ideal basis for their philosophy of the state, which was openly antagonistic to Machiavelli. Furthermore, and what is particularly to the point in our present investigation, they were all in one manner or another associated with the circle of Edmund Spenser.

Michel de l'Hôpital[47]

Born in Auvergne, de l'Hôpital studied at Toulouse and in the schools of law and letters at Padua. After the conclusion of his university career he filled various positions in and out of France: he was for a time at Rome,

---

[46] See below p. 69 f.

[47] In the following brief account of de l'Hôpital's life, I have relied chiefly upon Baudrillart, *op. cit.* See further A. F. Villemain, *Vie du Chancelier de l'Hôpital*, Paris, 1874; St. René Taillandier, *Le Chancelier de l'Hospital*, Paris, 1861; Dupré-Lasalle, *Michel de l'Hospital avant son élévation au poste de Chancelier de France*, Paris, 1875–1899; Amphoux, *Michel de l'Hospital et la liberté de conscience au XVI*ᵉ *siecle*, Paris, 1900; C. T. Atkinson, *Michel de l'Hospital*, London, 1900; A. E. Shaw, *Michel de l'Hospital and his Policy*, London, 1905; and the article in Eugene and Emile Haag's *La France protestante* (2nd Ed. 1877). Compare: du Bellay, *Au Seigneur de l'Hospital, Oeuvre Poétiques* (Soc. d. Textes Français Modernes, Ser. 1) vol. 2, p. 275; Ronsard, *A Michel de l'Hospital, Ode X, Oeuvres Complètes* (Bibliothèque Elzevirienne).

then at Bologna when the Council of Trent was sitting there. At one time Master of Requests and then President of the *Chambres des Comptes*, he finally attained in 1560 to the high office of Chancellor of France.

As Chancellor, de l'Hôpital was famous for his counsels of tolerance. The Edict of Romorantin, which was in the interest of those who stood within the danger of the Inquisition, had his support; as did the Edict of Orléans and that of January, 1562, which has been described as the most liberal, except the Edict of Nantes, which was ever granted to the Protestants of France. Other public acts attest equally well the spirit of the man. As an old man in his retirement at Vigny he was visited by Montaigne, about the time that the Massacres of St. Bartholomew's Eve were writing in blood the lessons of Ignatius Loyola; and when sending de l'Hôpital the Latin verses of Étienne de la Boétie, the philosophical sceptic paid this generouscompliment to the apostle of political tolerance: "I am anxious," said Montaigne, "to come and testify to you the honor and reverence with which I regard your competence and the special qualities which are in you; as for the extraneous and the fortuitous, it is not to my taste to put them in the account."[48]

In his *Traité de la Reformation de Justice*[49] de l'Hôpital has left us an eloquent exposition of the jurisprudence of the policists, which serves as an ideal background for what was by no means always a disinterested polity. To him as to Plato the first principle of justice is harmony, a principle which relates to the inner life as well as to the social and political ethic. "One must believe," says de l'Hôpital,[50] "that a man can not be just unless he is also magnanimous and courageous, temperate and full of prudence;[51] and this is true because justice is the harmony of all the other virtues; it is justice which lends them lustre and grace in full perfection, and it is justice which accomplishes them;" and "when the parts of

---

II, 68 ff., and Eclogue III, a *Chant Pastoral* in celebration of the marriage of Charles, Duke of Lorraine, and Madame Claude, daughter of Henry II, in which de l'Hospital appears as Michau, Du Bellay and Ronsard being represented by Bellot and Perrot respectively. For the friendship between Ronsard and de l'Hospital, see particularly Pierre de Nolhac, *Documents Nouveaux sur la Pléiade*, *Revue d'Histoire Littéraire de la France*, VI (1899), 351 ff. Michel de l'Hôpital's connections with the Pléiade are not without significance in our attempt to show that his philosophy of justice was congenial with the thought of Spenser. Note his mediatory offices in the literary as well as the political sphere: de Nolhac, *op. cit.*; *Critical Edition of the Discours de la Vie de Ronsard* by Claude Binet, Helene M. Evers, Appendix II. For criticism of Dr. Evers' dissertation, see Laumonier, *La Vie de P. de Rousard de Claude Binet*, *Édition Critique*, Paris, 1910, 134 ff.

[48] Courbet and Royer, *Les Essais de Montaigne*, IV, 299.

[49] In *Oeuvres de l'Hôpital*, ed. P. J. S. Dufey, 5 vols., Paris, 1824–1825. I might easily have extended the present section by a consideration of de l'Hôpital's other celebrated work, the *But de la guerre et de la paix*. What I have given here, however, seems to be sufficient for my purpose.

[50] *Op. cit.*, I, 110 ff.

[51] Conversely without justice the other virtues fail, *op. cit.*, I, 93.

the soul are so well regulated and composed that they produce in us prudence, temperance, and magnanimity, then there is formed and established a very beautiful and harmonious justice in man which causes him to approach the divine nature, when each part of his soul has that which belongs to it."[52] "Let us seek then first this accord, this consonance and this harmony in ourselves, since it is the cause of so great a good and tranquillity in our consciences, and since it unites us with God, a union in which consists the sovereign good of man." "Moreover," de l'Hôpital continues, "we should do all in our power to extend this principle of harmony to the body politic to the end that each one being content with his own and at peace with his neighbour, God should be served according to his will and the purity of his word. The end of justice is that the king should be obeyed, magistrates revered, and individuals protected in their goods, their lives, their honors, both they and their families according to their conditions, rank, and merits. God wills this by his goodness and mercy."[53]

Justice thus regarded as fundamental to the personal and political ethic is also considered as universal. Precisely as it is the same sun that shines at Paris as that which shines at Rome and Constantinople, so divine justice and natural right is no other among the savages of America than among the Christians of Europe. So far as human laws are concerned

[52] The contrast between the politic of de l'Hôpital and that of Machiavelli is suggested in the following passage:—"Je me soubviens d'avoir ouy aultre fois jargonner les rodomons et bravaches et belle happelourdes (faulx diamans) qui ont trouvé dans la science de leur bonne morgue (et c'est tout leur sçavoir, lequel se peult apprendre en moins d'une heure), que tout chrestien leur doibt foy et hommaige, à cause de leur belle mine et apparence, dient, pour magnifiques raisons, que, par la loy de nature, les gros poissons mangent les petits, les loups et aultres bestes ravissantes, les aigles, les faulcons, les vautours et aultres oyseaulx de proye mangent les oyseaulx qui ont peu de force et de résistance, et ainsy des aultres; et par ces raisons princes des bestes brutes, veulent prendre droict pour gourmander, injurier, forcer les ames innocentes, les hommes qui bien souvent valent cent fois mieulx qu' eulx, et qui ne payent pas le monde de mines, mais d'une bien plus forte monnoie et de beaucoup meilleur alloy, qui est l'intégrité, la sincérité de moeurs, la prudence, la justice et la saincte trouppe des aultres vertus" (Traité, II, 47–48). Compare Traité I, 93–94:—"Mais passons oultre, et considérons que les aultres vertus sans la justice sont manques et deffectueuses au possible? Premièrement qu'est ce aultre chose la magnanimité, la vaillantise et grandeur de couraige que l'homme injuste et meschant? Toute ceste hardiesse dont il faict parade et monstre intérieure n'est qu'ung fard, une mine, une apparence, ou du moins une présomption, audace et témérité qui rebouche aux périls tout ainsy qu'une lame de plomb contre une pierre dure, et que la vraye générosité, valeur et prouesse ne peult estre qu'en ung homme de bien et craignant Dieu. . . . Qui peult imaginer ung plus grand couraige en apparence qu'au Scythe Tamerlan, terreur de l'univers? Et neantmoins, parce qu'il n'y avoit poinct de justice en son faict, ceste hardiesse, ce hault couraige est plus tost imputé à une fureur bestiale qu' à une vraye génerosité."—The "saige mondain" without virtue is a hundred times more dangerous than a fool; Traité, I, 110.

[53] "Comme de vray, on ne sçauroit désirer ung plus heureux estre en ce monde que soubs l'estat monarchique et royal, royalement gouverné: soubs ce mot, la justice que est la vraye vertu royale, est comprinse, comme l'injustice n'est propre que pour les tyrans et oppresseurs du genre humain" (Traité, I, 244).

each people, monarch and sovereign will of course establish them according to the particular conveniences and necessities of province, country, and city. But in any case reason must be the soul of the law. Otherwise it cannot last, no more than the body can subsist without the soul.[54]

When de l'Hôpital contends that reason is the life of the law, he is far from recommending a merely rationalized politic. He argues, on the contrary, that the law of man is inseparable from the law of God, that justice is always attended by piety, injustice by impiety.[55] A corner-stone of his speculative piety is the dictum that the good Christian and the good citizen are one. He declares that no man who has the fear of God wishes that which belongs to another; nor will he withhold from God that which belongs to him. He will do unto others only as he would that others should do unto him. This it is to do justice and to accomplish in so doing the first commandment of the law of God.[56]

The Christian Platonism of de l'Hôpital's politic is further developed by his provision for the rôle of love in the execution of justice. "The remedies for injustice," he writes, "in the second book of the *Traité*, "are in our possession." "The fires which God will kindle if we implore his aid and his favor in the proper manner, the fires which will drive away the contagious air of injustice, are the fires of love, of charity towards our neighbors, which should warm the soul of every good man, but particularly the souls of Christians." Speaking of the French king, he declares: "Our true Aesculapius will be should it please him our hero and victorious prince, not less just than valiant, not less gracious and jealous of the love of his good subjects than a harsh ruler and enemy of rebels; not less pitiful toward the afflicted than a severe avenger of the proud, the violent, and the oppressors of the people."[57]

To keep the balance true between justice and mercy we should imitate God and love our fellow-men. The true judge, like the good shepherd, thinks of the people as committed to his charge.[58] Clemency, however,

[54] *Traité*, I, 60–61.
[55] Those who are not governed by piety and justice instead of following reason give the bridle to cupidities and unreasonable appetites (*Traité*, I, 132–3). Compare de la Noue, *Discours*, p. 3:—"Les saincts escrits font mention de trois pechez remarquables entre tous autres, qui le plus souvent se recontrent et joignent ensemble: à cause de quoy Dieu dissipe les Estats par punitions et ruines publiques: à savoir l'impieté, l'injustice et la dissolution." On page 6 of the *Discours* de la Noue declares that the Wars of Religion have made atheists. Compare further de la Noue, *Discours*, p. 513:—"Il (Plutarch) adjouste apres: Or, comme disoit Diogenes, tout est aux dieux, et toutes choses sont communes entre amis, et les bons sont amis des dieux: aussi est-il impossible que ceux qui sont devots et amis des dieux ne soyent quand et quand bienheureux, ni qu'un homme qui est vertueux, comme temperant et juste, ne soit aussi devot et religieux. N'est ce pas la trop bien parlé pour un Payen, qui jamais n'avoit en que fausses instructions?"
[56] *Op. cit.*, I, 21–22.
[57] *Op. cit.*, II, 9.
[58] "Nous demeurons à ces termes, que l'homme injuste ne faict rien et ne travaille que pour soy mesme, comme font ordinairement tous les tyrans, qui croyent en leur doctrine que

should not be inconsistent with severity. There is nothing that insures public peace and tranquillity more than the integrity of a great judge and the severity of his judgments; the judge assisted in the case of a monarchy by a righteous prince, who acts worthily in never pardoning the wicked and evil livers, and in making himself humane and helpful to good people.[59] "*Severitas senatorum pudoris et modestiae magistra; simul atque vel tantillum intermittur, statim obrepit indulgentia, petulantiae ac intemperantiae mater, scelerumque pene omnium fomes et receptaculum.*"[60] Mercy, on the other hand, is not only becoming to princes, magistrates and judges but is even necessary, provided that one has always regard to justice and that one uses justice and mercy so that one never appears without the other. All those who govern the republic ought always to abide in honorable moderation.[61] That is the natural seat of virtue. Extremes are always vicious. Justice should stand as it were in the midst of mercy and ever attended by it. Never under the pretext of mercy should we work injustice, nor under the protection of a harsh and severe justice should we be guilty of any cruelty. Justice and Mercy are like inseparable sisters. Those who are inspired with a zeal for piety and justice might well keep in mind the counsels of Seneca: "*Legum praesidem, ait, civitatisque rectorem decet, quamdiu potest, verbis, et iis mollibus, ingenia curare, ut facienda suadeat, cupiditatemque honesti et aequi conciliat animi, faciatque vitiorum odium, pretium virtutum: transeat deinde ad tristiorem orationem, qua moneat adhuc et exprobet; novissime ad poenas, et has adhuc leves et revocabiles decurrat: ultima supplicia ultimis sceleribus ponat, ut nemo pereat, nisi quem perire etiam pereuntis intersit.*"[62]

The nature and province of clemency as explained by de l'Hôpital substantially agree, as I understand the matter, with the description of that virtue in Seneca's *De Clementia*. Clemency, Seneca defines, as a modera-

---

le peuple est faict pour eulx. La Justice faict aultrement; elle n'a esgard qu'à ce qui appartient à aultruy pour le luy distribuer, à l'instar du bon roy, du fidèle tuteur, du soigneux berger, qui sçavent bien qu'ils sont constitués en leurs charges, non pour l'amour d'eulx mesmes et pour passer leur temps en délices et oysivetés, mais pour avoir soing et pourveoir au bien et utilité, l'ung de ses subjects, l'autre de son pupils et le tiers de son troupeau."—*Traité*, I, 75–76.

[59] *Op. cit.*, II, 174. Compare *Traité*, I, 189:—"C'est aimer les hommes, d'avoir soing d'eulx, leur faire du bien et proficter à tous; ce que peuvent faire les princes, et c'est en quoy consiste leur grandeur; c'est imiter Dieu, de protéger les bons, et de remunérer chascung selon leurs mérites, et punir rigoureusement les grands crimes et meschans desplorez, pardonner aux faultes légères qui ne vont pas à la ruyne ny destruction de personnes."

[60] *Op. cit.*, I, 130.

[61] "Mais venons à la tempérance et continence. Ceste vertu, qui scait ranger les appétits sensuels et les cupidités à la raison, ne va jamais guères seule, ains a la magnanimité pour fidelle compaigne, et unies ensemble font bien souvent des merveilles."—*Traité*, I, 94.

[62] *Traité*, I, 185 ff.:—"Faictes miséricorde à l'homme sanguinaire, meschant et assassineur; c'est vous mesme qui coupez la gorge, meurtrissez et assassinez ceulx qui tomberont entre les cruelles mains de cest homme de sang, et vostre vie respondra de celles qui auront puis esté perdeues par vostre et affectée clémence et miséricorde."

tion of the mind, a leaning of the mind to lenity in exacting punishments.[63] Its opposite, he says, is not severity but *crudelitas*, which is an atrocity of the mind in exacting punishments. Clemency, then, is not so much what distinguishes the particular judicial act, which out of pity makes an exception to the rule; it is rather the proper and constant mood of the righteous judge, who exacts justice more in sorrow than in anger, a spirit which Portia says is above the sceptred sway, that is enthroned in the hearts of kings, that is an attribute of God himself. Mercy, Seneca says, is to be carefully distinguished from *misericordia*, which he describes as a vice of the mind.[64] The Lord, according to the Christian version of this Roman opinion, loveth whom he chasteneth.[65]

[63] This, to be sure, is only one of several definitions offered by Seneca. The passage in question reads:—"Clementia est temperantia animi in potestate ulciscendi vel lenitas superioris adversus inferiorem in constituendis poenis. Plura proponere tutius est, ne una finitio parum rem comprehendat et, ut ita dicam, formula excidat; itaque dici potest et inclinatio animi ad lenitatem in poena exigenda. Illa finitio contradictiones inveniet, quamvis maxime ad verum accedat, si dixerimus clementiam esse moderationem aliquid ex merita ac debita poena remittantem; reclamabitur nullam virtutem cuiquam minus debito facere. Atqui hoc omnes intellegunt clementiam esse, quae se flectit citra id, quod merito constitui posset.

"Huic contrariam inperiti putant severitatem; sed nulla virtus virtuti contraria est. Quid ergo obponitur clementiae? Crudelitas, quae nihil aliud est quam atrocitas animi in exigendis poenis." *De Clementia*, II, 3.

[64] "Ad rem pertinet quaerere hoc loco, quid sit misericordia; plerique enim ut virtutem eam laudant et bonum hominem vocant misericordem. Et haec vitium animi est."—Seneca, *De Clementia*, II, 4.

[65] I cannot forbear quoting at this point from de l'Hôpital the following eloquent description of the just man:—"L'homme juste, mesmement celuy qui est constitué en dignité, premièrement ne faict rien par ignorance, par erreur, par surprise, ne se laisse emporter par les artifices, inventions et imprudences d'ung hardy menteur et rusé calomniateur, par les afféteries non d'ung orateur que je tiens pour homme de bien, mais d'ung discoureur, d'ung babillard, je dirois voluntiers d'ung bavard charlatan, qui employe son estude à desguiser l'innocence et la vérité, s'efforce, par ses ruses, d'obtenir ce qu'il prétend en faveur du mensonge et de la calomnie; parce que la prudence luy faict fidelle compaignie, luy descouvre les subtilités, calomnies, ruses et impostures, de quelque part qu'elles viennent; et, s'il n'est pas assez instruict pour l'heure, il aime mieulx différer qu'en précipitant faire injustice, et attend jusques à ce que sa conscience soit informée et satisfaicte de tout poinct; ne faict rien aussy par flatteries, blandices [caresses], par faveurs, par amour, par hayne, par envie, par jalousie, par avarice, par tesmérité, ny oultre passion. Sa tempérance l'en empesche et tient les maulvaises cupidités asserviees soubs le joug de la raison; encore moins par orgueil, par présomption, par force, par craincte, par menaces, ny dangers quelconques, parce qu'il possède la vraye magnanimité, qui jamais ne l'abandonne et luy faict mespriser tous hazards, et aime mieulx perdre les biens temporels ou la vie mesme que de faire une injustice et meschanté, ou ne l'empescher de tout son pouvoir;

    Non civium ardor prava jubentium,
    Non vultus instantis tyranni
    Mente quatit . . . . *Op. cit.*, I, 194–195.

Compare de la Noue, *Discours*, p. 72: "Mais que celui qui juge le face en se conduisant selon les regles de charité. Car ceux qui condamnent les autres par orgueil, il avient apres que Dieu les condamne par justice."

François de la Noue

François de la Noue (1531-1591), often called *Bras-de-Fer* (a sobriquet due to the iron arm which he wore after his left arm had been shattered at the siege of Fontenoy), was one of the most prominent of the Huguenot captains during the period of the Religious Wars. A friend of Sir Philip Sidney, he devoted himself not only to the cause of the Rochellois but to the Protestant cause in the Netherlands. Captured by the Spaniards in 1580, he spent five years in a prison at Limboy, giving himself there to the composition of his *Discours politiques et militaires*,[66] which was first published at Basle in 1587. After he had been liberated in 1589, he returned to active warfare. Then he was wounded at the siege of Lambolle and died at Moncontour on the fourth of August, 1591.

La Noue, like de l'Hôpital, combined counsels of tolerance with a recognition of the claims of severity. Concord, he declares, is "le seul ciment qui peut rejoindre les membres de ce caduque et ancien edifice tout entr'ouvert" (Epistre III). But it is necessary to remember that there is a false as well as a true concord:[67] "Avant que finir ce discours-ci, il faut aussi parler de la fausse concorde, et paraventure qu'il ne nuira de rien de donner quelques petis advertissemens sur ce poinct, à fin qu'on ne soit abusé, comme ceux qui ont pris un faux escu pour un bon, par faute de le peser et bien regarder." In words similar, as we shall see to those of Bodin, he says that concord among pirates, robbers, and prostitutes is in reality "un secret discord, cimente de poison" (p. 62). Another kind of false concord is that of the German peasants who revolted against the nobles. This is a *concorde furieuse*. The parties to it, though living together like brothers and even dying together courageously, adopt purposes and procedures which are detestable. He classifies here the Anabaptists of Münster and the Sicilians in revolt against the French; "avec telles gens nous devons plustot avoir discord qu'accord: pour ce que leur union ne vise qu'à alterer les societez legitimes" (62-63). Somewhat further on la Noue speaks of four types of false concord:—*Concorde tyrannique*, exemplified by the rule of Caesar Borgia, "qui a esgalé les tyrans du passé en execrables meschancetez,—le beau patron que Machiavel propose, pour enseigner aux princes comment ils doyvent regner;" *concorde injuste*, an example of which is to be found in Rome under Nero, when senators and judges agreed to commit every iniquity; *concorde insolente*, which depends upon the dominance of the military class; and *concorde héretique* and *schismatique*, which united the Arian bishops who opposed the Council of Nice (64-66).

[66] *Discours politiques et militaires du Seigneur de la Noue. Nouvellement recueillis et mis en lumière à Basle. De l'Imprimerie de François Forest*, 1587.

[67] "Mais la concorde qui dure, est celle qui est entre les gens de bien, et qui procede des mouvements d'une droite raison illuminée d'en-haut, qui nous rend affectionnez au bien les uns des autres: car estant alimentee d'une humeur radicale si parfaite, elle demeure tousjours vive et fraische comme les arbres qui sont plantez au long des rivages des eaux courantes" (*Discours*, II, p. 66).

In maintaining the true as distinguished from the false types of concord, la Noue agrees with the opinion "qui mesle ensemble la douceur et la rigueur." The violent remedies which only aggravate the sickness should of course be rejected, but we should also avoid those which are too gentle to be effective.[68] "Ceux à qui les choses mauvaises desplaisent, quand ils voyent qu'avec trop de douceur et trop mollement on procede à les corriger, ils pensent qu'il y ait quelque secrete connivence avec icelles. —Qu'est-il donc de faire pour abolir ces petites guerres qui se font en paix, et qui rallument les haines et relevent les partialitez? C'est d'attrapper cinq ou six de ces guerriers, à fin que cinq ou six cents deviennent sages. Somme, puisque par la continuation des discussions civiles, l'audace, la malice, et la desobeissance sont si fort accreuës, on ne doit pas penser avec les edicts et ordonnances les pouvoir reprimer, si la verge n'est aussi en la main de ceux à qui il appartient de la porter, pour donner poids aux paroles. Et combien qu'en ceste reformation-ci considerant les choses en general, on y doyve proceder avecques beaucoup de moderation, à fin de ne rien esmouvoir ni troubler: si est-ce qu'en regardant en particulier plusieurs qualitez vicieuses, qui empeschent le restablissement de l'ordre il semble que ce n'est point erreur que de mesler avecques la douceur quelque portion de severité" (104-107).

I fancy it was not only de la Noue's philosophy of justice which might have attracted Spenser to the *Discours*. The principle that "les gentil-shommes doyvent estre ornez de plusieurs vertus" he discusses at some length in his *Dixième Discours* (198 ff.). This, which might be called the text of the *Faerie Queene*, justifies us in associating the book with those treatises dealing with the education of a courtier of which our poet's great allegory is confessedly a poetical version. "Les peintres," de la Noue writes, "ont accoustumé de peindre les Muses toutes en une troupe, qui ne s'abandonnent point. Avec aussi bonne raison pourroyent-ils faire le mesme de ceste digne societé, en laquelle les associez se plaisent fort de demorrer: d'où nous devons titer enseignment, qui puisque si volontairement elles se rengent ensemble, aussi nous leur devons tousjours tenir nostre porte ouverte, à fin que l'une y estant entree, elle attire les autres apres. Je sçay bien que la fortitude (qu'on dit estre prouesse ou vaillance) est une excellente vertu, propre tant aux grands qu'aux petis, et sans laquelle la vie des uns et des autres est molle et sans vigueur: mais si elle est destituee de justice, elle est nuisible aux bons. Si la temperance ne la modere, elle se tournera en foureur: et n'estant guidee par prudence elle agira mal à propos. En quoy on void qu'il y a une liaison entr'elles, et une

---

[68] "Ceste charité, de quoy je parle, ne contrevient point à la justice civile, et n'abolit l'indignation que nous devons avoir contre les contempteurs de Dieu: car si elle contrarioit à la pieté et à l'ordre public, elle ne seroit humaine, ains inhumaine. Et y a bonne proportion entre elle et la divine: d'autant que l'une dit, Tu aimeras Dieu de tout ton coeur; et l'autre, Tu aimeràs ton prochain comme toy-mesme (*Discours*, p. 77).

aide mutuelle qu'elles s'entrefont: qui ne se pourroit alterer qu'au prejudice de chacune en particulier. Les mariniers estiment qu'une seule anchre n'est pas suffisante pour tenir ferme et arrester un navire. Autant en pourroit-on dire des nobles, qu'il faut plus d'une virtu pour donner fermeté à leur reputation. Ce qui bien connu de ceux qui sont instituez en la doctrine morale, dont le nombre est bien petit, à cause que l'erreur, de quoy nous traitons, a rendu trop partiale la plus grande multitude. Cela se void aucunement aux titres que plusieurs se baillent, s'appelans les bras de la patrie, les gardiens des armes, et la terreur des ennemis: qui sont titres que je ne reprouve pas. Toutefois il me semble que se dire, professeurs de vertu, comprendroit encores plus, et les honnereroit davantage." One should note too la Noue's praise of country life as contrasted with that of courts and cities as doubtless pleasing to the author of *Colin Clout*.[69]

Jean Bodin

Jean Bodin was born at Angers in 1529 or 1530.[70] The tradition that his mother was a Jewess, though lacking confirmation, is of interest in connection with his knowledge of Hebrew and his unquestionable sympathy with Hebraic culture. He studied like de l'Hôpital at Toulouse, and later he delivered lectures there. The immediate fruit of his legal studies, such as the *De Decretis* and the *De Imperio*, are preserved to us only by title; and we know little of the years that he spent after leaving Toulouse as an unsuccessful barrister at Paris. To his failure to meet the practical demands of his profession and to his love of scholarship we owe the books that have made him famous.

[69] See the chapter in the *Discours* (196 ff.) entitled "De Trois Fausses Opinions lesquelle font desvoyer plusieurs de la Noblesse."

[70] For the life of Bodin see particularly Baudrillart, *Jean Bodin et Son Temps*, Paris, 1853; Barthélemy, *Étude sur Jean Bodin*, Paris, 1876, in the Publications of the Société académique de Saint-Quentin; Jean Chauviré, *Jean Bodin, auteur de la 'République,'* Paris, 1915; and the article "Bodin" in Julius Bachem's *Staatslexicon, Zweite Auflage*, I, 946 ff. In my sketch of Bodin's life I have followed Baudrillart rather closely. For Bodin's relations to Judaism, see, Rabbin Guttman, *J. Bodin in seinem Beziehungen zum Judentum*, Breslau, 1906. Upon the disputed matter of Bodin's religion Chauviré in his *Jean Bodin*, 258 f., writes: "On peut apprendre enfin, d'une pareille étude, ce que la seule lecture de la *République* laisse encore indécis, à savoir quel est le parti de Bodin. 'Je ne parle point icy, dit-il quelque part, laquelle des religions est la meilleure (combien qu'il n'y a qu'une religion, une verité, une loy divine publiée par la bouche de Dieu).' Mais nous savons à présent que la meilleure à ses yeux n'est point la catholique, puisqu'il ne s'inspire, tout en en combattant les excès, que des libelles de tendance huguenote. Ou bien Bodin est protestant, ou bien, s'il ne l'est plus, il est arrivé à cette religion naturelle, teintée de judaïsme, que l'*Heptaplomeres* recommandra. Quant au parti qu'il embrasse, la chose est encore plus claire. Politique, il est à l'aile droite des Politiques, c'est à dire qu'il s'appuie sur les huguenots et leur arguments pour conquérir ou défendre les libertés nécessaires, mais qu'il répudie les principes excessifs qui méconnaîtraient l'autorité royale, à son avis seul garant de l'ordre national. En attendant, et pour garder à cette autorité son prestige intact, que le prince ne persécute plus ses sujets pour cause de religion. Et paix dans les deux religions aux hommes de bonne volonté."

The first of these is the *Methodus ad facilem historiarum cognitionem*, which was published in 1566. This justly celebrated work and the *Response aux paradoxes de M. de Malestroit touchant le fait des monnoies et l'enchérissement de toutes choses*, which appeared two years later, seem to have opened to Bodin a way to preferment. At any rate by 1571 he has become *maître de requêtes* and the adviser of the Duke d'Alençon, already the acknowledged leader of *les politiques*. In the same year as king's attorney he defended under the law of *Tiers et Danger* the inalienable right of the crown to the royal domain in Normandy against the claims of four hundred noble families—a position which Bodin maintained even after Charles IX. had yielded to the determined opposition of the nobles. Though there is insufficient evidence to prove that Bodin was a Protestant, his principles of tolerance marked him as an enemy of all strict Catholics; so that it was only with difficulty that he saved his life during the Massacre of St. Bartholomew. For some time after this he stayed away from Paris. Upon his return we find him enjoying for a period the favour of Henry III., who held his learning in high esteem. In 1576 he is king's attorney at Laon and a deputy of the *tiers-état* at Blois. The proceedings of the estates at this place are recorded by Bodin himself in his *Recueil de tout ce qui s'est negocié en la compagnie du tiers-états de France en l'assemblee generale des trois états, assignee par le roi en la ville de Blois au 15 novembre 1576*.

At Blois the chief question was that of religious unity to be attained at any cost as opposed to the policy of conciliation between Catholicism and Calvinism. Versoris spoke for strong repression of the reformed religion; Bodin, for conciliation; and, although the latter's counsels of tolerance did not prevail, they are of interest as an application in public life of opinions which his books have developed and defended on philosophical grounds. With this advocacy of religious tolerance there goes a devotion to the political institutions of his country. He was loyal to the monarchy to the extent of incurring the displeasure of the king, as appears in his opposition to the alienation of the royal domain to meet the expenses of the realm. This position and his championship of the traditional rights of the estates cost him the favour of Henry III.

Bodin now associates himself more closely with the Duke d'Alençon, who had become the Duke d'Anjou, and who was still regarded as the leader of *les politiques*. In the retinue of this prince he goes to England. He finds that his *Republic* is well known at Cambridge; and while at the University he meets Gabriel Harvey, to whom he appears to have shown some special favour. Queen Elizabeth playfully dubs him *Badin* because of the raillery with which she thought he had written of women. Later Bodin accompanies the Duke to the Low Countries, continuing in his service until the death of Anjou in 1584. He then returns to Laon and becomes in 1587 the successor of his father-in-law in the office of *procureur général*. About this time there occurred an event which Baudrillart calls "un épisode regrettable," "si contraire à tous ses principes." It was in a word Bodin's surprising declaration of adherence to the Holy League. "Le philosophe," writes Baudrillart, "et, sauf cette courte eclipse, l'homme public furent toujours ou se trouvaient la nationalité et la tolerance."[71] In spite of his formal allegiance to the League, Bodin's conduct continued to be so little to the liking of that party that in 1590 he was accused of heresy, his lodgings searched, and his books publicly burned. In 1593, three years before his death, he did something to atone for his past error by a public declaration in favour of Henry IV.

The first of Bodin's works which require our attention is his *Methodus ad facilem historiarum cognitionem*, published in 1566.[72] Anticipating Montesquieu[73] at many points, our author emphasises the bearing of the the history of law upon the record of human events. But as history is to him not simply human but natural and divine history as well, so law is something higher and broader than statutes and codes. To find the constant terms among the shifting factors of his problem, the historian must turn to Nature and God. Following the stages of the mystic quest he should consider first himself, in the second place the family, in the third place civil society, then nature, and finally God. Only a few men, however, are capable of thus rising above the senses, as the swimmer with effort keeps his head above water.

Chapter VI of the *Methodus (De Statu Rerumpublicarum)*, in which the author anticipates ideas later developed in the *Republic*, discusses particularly Platonic communism. "Je ne crois pas," writes Baudrillart, "qu'on ait jamais dit sur ce sujet controversé rien de plus net et de plus vigoureux: changez quelques mots à peine et vous croiriez entendre un philosophe ou un publiciste de nos jours."[74] The hypothesis of Plato, Bodin argues, is radically false; for Nature teaches us that this world, an admirable work of God, consists of unequal parts and of elements which are in sharp conflict one with another, and that the various movements of the stars are so necessary to maintain the world that without this harmonic discord everything would perish. And the most politic state, if it imitates Nature as it should, will preserve the inequalities of governors and governed, of masters and servants, of rich and poor, of good and wicked, of strong and weak; a certain mélange of opposed minds helps to preserve the integrity of the state.

---

[71] Baudrillart, *op. cit.*, 131 ff.

[72] I have used the Paris edition of 1572, and the analysis of the *Methodus* given by Fritz Renz in Lamprecht's *Geschichtliche Untersuchungen, Dritter Band, Erstes Heft*, Gotha, 1905: *Jean Bodin, Ein Beitrag zur Geschichte des historischen Methode im 16 Jahrhundert*. Robert Flint in his *Historical Philosophy in France* (New York, 1894) summarizes the treatise. See, too, Chauviré, *op. cit.*, 294 ff.

[73] Fournol, *Bodin, prédécesseur de Montesquieu*, 1896.

[74] Baudrillart, *op. cit.*, 155.

Having introduced the parallel of harmonized voices, Bodin concludes that thanks to the upper, lower, and middle classes, the state finds an accord in a happy combination of opposites.

The true state, Bodin contends here and later in the *Republic*, is monarchical. This form of government is as natural as the communistic state is unnatural. Why should we not conform here as elsewhere to the example of Nature? The monarchical principle is illustrated on every hand in the world about us. Animals such as bees and cattle follow a chief; and in the world of inanimate objects there is always something which excels all others, as gold among the metals, the sun among the stars. Finally there is only one God, the lord and maker of the world. If then Nature cries out against communism, if reason revolts against it, if long experience testifies against it, why should we prefer Plato to the nature of things.

Bodin is, however, in the *Methodus* concerned not so much with the philosophy of the state as with the method of the historian. And from this point of view the book is of importance in the present investigation because, although Spenser and Bodin are not in agreement at all points, the historical method which is expounded by the French publicist was certainly familiar to the English poet.

The uncertain and confused nature of human affairs our writer concedes makes impossible in historical investigations the exact methods of mathematics and the natural sciences.[75] Accordingly the historian has to content himself with an approximation to truth: *Historiae naturales verae sint necne facillime intelliguntur; humanae vero, quae semper sui dissimiles sunt, non item.*[76] Corresponding to the differences of subject matter in human, natural, and religious history, he postulates an *assensio triplex, probabilis, necessaria, religiosa*.[77] Nevertheless the history of man adopts as its chief purpose the attainment of truth, and it must accordingly rest upon reliable sources. The historian who bases his narrative upon the documents themselves necessarily carries more authority than one who takes his material second hand.[78] Nor should an historian rest his case upon a single record. Documents should be collated[79] and the learning, prejudices, religion, etc. of the historian should be taken into account in assessing the value of his

---

[75] "Aut si quis nolit cum naturalibus disciplinis mathematicas confundere, quatuor genera constituet historiarum: humanam quidem incertam et confusam: naturalem certam, interdum tamen materiae vel mali genii contagione incertam ac sui dissimilem: mathematicam quod a concretione materiae libera sit, certiorem: sic enim veteres hanc ab illa diviserunt. Postremum divinam certissimam et sui natura plane immutabilem. Atque haec de historiarum partitione" (*Methodus*, I, 17 f.).

[76] Renz, *op. cit.*, 15.

[77] *Methodus*, Chapter I, 11; Renz, *op. cit.*, 16.

[78] Renz, *op. cit.*, 17.

[79] Renz, *op. cit.*, 28.

report.[80] History of past times and of foreign peoples, having more detachment, is in many ways more reliable than that of contemporaries and natives;[81] and oral tradition is generally to be viewed with suspicion.[82]

Bodin's method, as we have noted, however scientific it might be, did not put history out of touch with other subjects. This would have been impossible for one who was as interested as he in unifying the diversity of human experience. He combines in a striking manner the mystic and the rational temper, and strives for an articulation of the many sided life of man. Accordingly he was concerned not only to survey and define the province of history but to correlate it with law and philosophy. Moreover, physiology, psychology, and physical geography, in helping us to understand the character of a people will enable us the better to read or write its history. In all that he says of the significance of the milieu, Bodin harks back to mediaeval lore of the relations of the material body to the immaterial soul and he anticipates much later speculation with which everyone associates the name of Hippolyte Taine.[83]

The character of the folk or race, constituting a part of the historian's subject, will be understood by attention not only to the physical milieu but to the mixture of races, which has often brought about an alteration of a people's customs. For instance in their union with the Britons, the Danes, Angles, and Saxons have made those people more warlike, while they themselves have become more cultivated. Such changes, of course, will come about slowly in the case of races which, though living side by side, do not mingle with one another.[84]

Bodin's recognition of the differences of racial character, due to milieu and race mixture, leads him to the position that there should be a careful adaptation of laws and institutions to the special character of the people for whom they are intended.[85] Accordingly he denies the possibility of an ideal state, of validity for all people; for what would be useful for one people would be harmful to another.[86] The differing character of historical periods also receives recognition in this connection, the state at any given time being considered the result of organic development, and the growth of the state corresponding to that of a man from childhood through maturity to decay and death.[87]

Such a far perspective naturally turned the attention of Bodin to the question of the origin of races.[88] His method in dealing with this subject

---

[80] Renz, *op. cit.*, 22 ff.
[81] Renz, *op. cit.*, 27, 29.
[82] Renz, *op. cit.*, 17, 19.
[83] Renz, *op. cit.*, 38 ff. Compare, *passim*, A. J. Koller, *The Theory of Environment*, 1918.
[84] Renz, *op. cit.*, 66 ff.
[85] Renz, *op. cit.*, 62.
[86] Renz, *op. cit.*, 62.
[87] Renz, *op. cit.*, 63.
[88] Renz, *op. cit.*, 66 ff.

deserves our attention. As sources of evidence he recognizes historical documents, philological characteristics, and geography. From the first of these his scientific method can expect little, but he has a good deal to say about the value of philological and geographical considerations.

In support of the testimony of Moses, Herodotus, and Xenophon that the Chaldeans were the oldest race, the Hebrew language being only a dialect of Chaldean, he seeks to trace to a Babylonian-Hebrew origin the names of all peoples. His descent is by a pretty uncomfortable route from Chaldean, Hebrew, and Egyptian to Greek and then to Italian. The Celts, too, he attempts to show are descendants of the Greeks, and the Germans of the Celts. The great differences which the languages of these people have developed are due to the passage of time, colonization, and race mixture, and to the influence of milieu.

Considering in the large the evolution of the civilization of the world, Bodin as a scientific historian can give little comfort to the poet's dream of a golden age which the world had outlived. All the evidence, he declares, is against such a view. The cycles of time are cycles of growth and decay, but the wheel of change is ever ascending the hill of progress; or, to use his figure, the field grows in fertility with the decay of vegetation. *Haec illa est rerum omnium tam certa conversio, ut dubitare nemo debeat, quin idem in hominum ingeniis quid in agris eveniat, qui majori ubertate gratiam quietis referre solent.*[89]

After the *Methodus*, Bodin published in 1568 his *Response de Jean Bodin aux Paradoxes de M. de Malestroit, touchant le fait des Monnaies et l'Enchérissment de Toutes Choses*. Then followed in 1576, the year in which he was appointed king's attorney at Laon, the *Six Livres de la République*,[90] a work of the first importance in the political speculations of the sixteenth century.

In his preface addressed to Monseigneur Du Faur, Bodin (pp. 2-3) compares his book with the similar works of Plato, Aristotle, and Machiavelli. The works of Plato and Aristotle are cut too short, he thinks, to satisfy the appetites of those who read them. Besides the time that has elapsed since those great men wrote has brought much to light that was hidden from them; even Plato confesses that the subject is very obscure. Others who have followed them have profaned the sacred mysteries of political philosophy in their ignorance of law and even of public justice. We have for instance a Machiavelli, who has enjoyed a vogue among the

---

[89] Renz, *op. cit.*, 71 ff.
[90] I have used the Paris edition of 1577. The analysis and summary of the *Republic* in Baudrillart, *op. cit.*, I have found very helpful. For a briefer digest, see Bluntschli, *Geschichte der neueren Staatswissenschaft*, München und Leipzig, 1881 (Third Edition), Chapter II. A careful examination of the sources of the Republic and a much more dispassionate account of Bodin in general than that of Baudrillart will be found in the excellent book of Jean Chauviré already mentioned.

courtiers of tyrants, and whom Paulus Jovius, while placing him in the rank of distinguished men describes nevertheless as an atheist and one ignorant of good literature. As for atheism Machiavelli glories in it in his writings; and so far as his knowledge is concerned, "ceux qui ont accoustumé de discourir doctement, pezer sagement, et resoudre subtilement les hauts affaires d'estat, s'accorderont qu'il n'a jamais sondé le gué de la science Politique, qui ne gist pas en ruzes tyranniques, qu'il a recherchees par tous les coins d'Italie, et comme une douce poizon coulee en son livre du Prince, où il rehausse jusques au Ciel, et met pour un Parangon de tous les Roys, le plus desloyal filz de Prestre qui fut oncques: et lequel neantmoins avec toutes ses finesses, fut honteusement precipité de la roche de tyrannie haute et glissante, où il s'estoit niché, et en fin exposé comme un belistre à la mercy et risee de ses ennemis, comme il est advenu depuis aux autres Princes qui ont suyvi sa piste, et pratiqué les belles reigles de Macciavel; lequel a mis pour deux fondemens des Republiques l'impieté et l'injustice, blasant la religion comme contraire à l'estat."

Bodin's hostility to Machiavelli so vigorously expressed in this passage, will help us to appreciate the natural antipathy of *la politique spiritualiste* for *la politique matérialiste*. Baudrillart speaks of Machiavelli as the adversary almost always present to Bodin. "Avec le publiciste français," he continues, "on peut dire que la politique spiritualiste prend à son tour la parole, et exerce de noble represailles contre la politique matérialiste alors dans toute sa vogue: mérite d'autant plus frappant qu'il s'allie ici à un esprit observateur et qui offre avec Machiavel lui-même une remarquable analogie par son caractère éminemment expérimental.—Aux maximes bien connues du Prince, il substitue les principes d'une morale élevée, principes éternels, jamais plus opportuns, et dont l'application à la politique n'allait à rien moins qu'à faire révolution dans les idées reçues et dans la pratique adoptée."[91]

But this anti-Machiavellism of *les politiques*, which was recognized by the dedication of Gentillet's *Anti-Machiavel* to the Duc d'Alençon after that nobleman had become associated with the party of Henry of Navarre, does not mean that the policists drifted to Utopian idealism. Bodin does not share the dreams of Plato and More, whose ideal states he regarded as republics "en idee sans effet."[92] What Bodin seeks is a practicable polity informed and inspired by ideals. The end of the political life is not happiness but virtue, and the highest virtue is realized in the life of contemplation. That republic, he says, will be deemed happy that numbers among

[91] Baudrillart, *op. cit.*, 225 ff. Compare de l'Hôpital, *op. cit.*, II, 12:—"Je ne suis pas figuré une réformation et réglement impossible, ni mesme difficile: je me soubviens des Respublicques de Platon, de la Cyropédie de Xénophon, de l'Utopie de Thomas Morus et aultres qui ont excellement discoureu, et miz par escript de belles et eslevées conceptions; mais ce sont fruicts qui n'estaient plus de saison."

[92] *République*, I, Chapter 1, p. 3.

its citizens many men whose lives illustrate the intellectual and contemplative virtues. The first book of his *Republic* sets forth unmistakably the mystical ethic in which his practical politic found its inspiration. The Republic should first of all provide the necessities of life.[93] But the good man will not be satisfied with what contributes to his needs and comforts; he will wish further to side with the virtuous against the wicked; and when his spirit is clear and swept clean of vices and passions which trouble the soul, he will observe more carefully the diversity of human things—various ages, contrary humors, the grandeur of some the ruin of others, the vicissitudes of republics—and he will seek always the causes of the effects which he has noted. Then after a time, turning to the beauty of nature, he will take pleasure in the variety of the animal, the vegetable, and the mineral world, considering of each thing its special form, its quality and its virtue; considering further the hostility and the friendships of creatures toward one another and how they are joined by the sequence of cause and effect. Then passing beyond elementary religion, he will preen the wings of contemplation for his heavenly flight, that he might see the splendor, the beauty, and the strength of the celestial luminaries, their magnificence and fearful motions, and that he might hear the melodious harmony of the whole world. He is then ravished with a wonderful pleasure and attended by a ceaseless desire to find the first cause, and him who was the author of such a beautiful work of art. Having reached this point he no longer pursues the course of his contemplation, inasmuch as the maker is infinite and incomprehensible in essence, in grandeur, in power, in wisdom, and in goodness. By this method of contemplation wise men have proved that there is only one God, eternal and infinite; and thence they have as it were drawn a conclusion of human happiness.[94]

With the passage just summarized should be compared the paragraph that closes the first chapter of the first book: Bodin here compares the soul ravished in contemplation and burning with divine brightness to the

[93] Irenaeus in the *Veue* argues that in the reformation of Ireland the care of the body should precede that of the soul; *Veue* p. 646.

[94] *République*, Book I, Ch. 1:—With this passage should be compared the following from the *Methodus*:—"Quoniam hominibus primum studium conservandi sui natura parens ingeneravit: deinde paulatim a rerum naturalium admiratione ad causarum investigationem impulit: tum ab iis illecebris ad ipsius rerum omnium moderatoris cognitionem pertraxit: ob eam causam ab historia rerum humanarum nobis auspicandum videtur, cum primum de summo Deo comprehensiones, non solum probabiles, sed etiam ad assentiendum necessariae in puerorum animis radices egerint. Ita fiet ut a cogitatione nostri primum, deinde familiae, tum communis societatis ad naturę inspectionem, ac postremo ad immortalis Dei veram historiam, id est, contemplationem, abducamur."—*Methodus*, Cap. primum, pp. 12-13. See, too, *Methodus*, Cap. tertium, 33 ff.:—"Et quoniam primum studium conservandi sui natura unicuique ingeneravit, primae hominum actiones ad ea pertinent, sine quibus vivi nullo modo potest: deinde ad ea sine quibus vivi quidem, sed non satis commode; aut commode, sed non splendide; aut splendide, non tamen ad eam, quae suavissime sensus oblectat, voluptatem: hinc opum augendarum cupiditas. Sed quia voluptatum nulla satietas, aut ea communis est

moon reflecting the glory of the sun. The soul given too much to the pleasures of the body, the soul that does not seek the divine sun, he compares to the moon hid by the shadows of the earth, which having robbed it of its light and its strength, brings forth in its stead many monsters. "Et neantmoins si elle demeuroit tousjours unie au soleil, il est bien certain que le monde elementaire periroit. Nous ferons mesme jugement de la Republique bien ordonnnee, la fin principale de laquelle gist aux vertus contemplatives, jaçoit que les actions politiques soient preallables, et les moins

beluarum aeque ac hominum, quo quisque generosior est, eo longius se a beluarum societate disiungit, ac paulatim gloriae cupiditate fertur, ut reliquis praestare possit: hinc dominandi libido, et tenuioribus vis illata, hinc dissidia, bella, servitutes, caedes. Sed cum hoc vitę genus turbulentum sit ac periculis plenum, tum vero immanis ea gloria quae hominem excelsi animi explere non possit, consequens est ut homo bene a natura informatus, paulatim feratur ad virtutis actiones, quae in vera laude et solida gloria versantur, in qua plerique finem extremum constituunt. Sed quoniam natura quietis est appetens, planum est eas virtutis actiones ad quietem aliquando dirigi oportere. Quo fit ut homo paulatim a curis et hominum societate distractus solitudinem querat, ut tranquillitate naturae consentanea fruatur. Itaque res humanas despiciens earumque inconstantiam ac temeritatem, naturae causas certissimas intuetur, in quibus contemplandis tantam percipit voluptatem, ut talium studiorum conscientia fretus, regum opes ac Fortunas negligat: quinetiam plerique cum maxima imperia gessissent, ad hoc vitae genus sponte relabi, quam regnare maluerunt. Hinc illae scientiae ac virtutes, quae quod in veri sola cognitione acquiescunt, θεορικαι vocantur. Neque vero id satis est homini bene a natura instituto, ut in iis scientiis, quarum subjecta materia sub sensum cadit, acquiescat; sed his veluti gradibus ad ea fertur, quae sola mente percipiuntur, id est, ad animorum immortalium vim ac potestatem, quousque pernicibus alis sursum abripiatur, ac suae originis primordia repetens, cum Deo penitus conjungatur; in quo finis humanarum actionum et quies extrema, summaque fœlicitas consistit. Huc omnia consilia, dicta, facta: huc humanae actiones, huc disciplinae ac virtutes referuntur.

Like Bodin, de la Noue is interested in the relation of the contemplative to the active life; for example, *Discours*, p. 533:—"Voila comment la vie contemplative ne doit point estre desjointe, ni pour tousjours, ni pour long temps de l'active. Ce que mesme les meilleurs Philosophes ont bien connu. Et ce grand Theologien, S. Augustin, a approuvé du tout ceste bien ordonnee composition de l'une et de l'autre. Car encores que les actions spirituelles soyent plus dignes que les corporelles, toutes on ne les doit pas separer." Further, *Discours*, p. 540 (Compare Spenser's treatment of the subject at the close of the first book of the Faerie Queene):—"Quelqu'un dira, encores que le Philosophe doive contempler, que pourtant il ne semble pas que le Prince, le Capitaine, le Juge et le Medecin ayent grand besoin de s'y travailler: pource qu'on ne requiert d'eux seulement que de bons effects. Je respondray qu'iceux effects procedent des bonnes consultations, et les consultations de la prudence, à laquelle on parvient premierement par experience: puis par meditation." Again, *Discours*, pp. 539–540:- "Celui qui considerera le parler, qui est seulement propre à l'homme, pensera qu'il n'y a rien qui soit si commun et familier: mais s'il monte jusques à la parole intérieure, qui est la conception de l'entendement, auquel receptacle mille images parfaites, fausses et vrayes resident, passent et repassent, qui se manifestent apres par la parole sensible, il admirera un si haut ouvrage de Dieu. Et en ceste maniere devons nous des choses corporelles monter aux incorporelles: et des plus hautes retourner apres aux basses. Car qu'est-ce autre chose que la composition de l'homme, sinon le celeste, et le terrestre, qui par un artifice tres-excellent et inimitable sont conjoints ensemble? Dequoy on peut tirer ceste instruction, que la vie contemplative et l'active convienent tres bien l'une avecques l'autre: et les vouloir du tout separer, c'est comme vouloir faire force à nature."

illustres soient les premieres: comme faire provisions necessaires, pour entretenir et defendre la vie des sujets; et neantmoins telles actions se rapportent aux morales, et celles cy aux intellectuelles, la fin desquelles est la contemplation du plus beau sujet qui soit, et qu'on puisse imaginer." This order of life is that which God ordained when he set aside six days of the week for work and the seventh for the contemplation of his works and his law and for his praise. Here then is the principal end of republics well conducted, which are the happier the nearer they approach this end. In republics as in men there are several degrees of felicity; some have more, others less according to the end which each has proposed for itself. One might say, for example, of the Lacedemonians that they were courageous and magnanimous, but that nevertheless their actions were unjust, for the reason that their institutions and laws had no other object than that of making men brave and invincible. But the Roman republic has flourished in justice and surpassed that of the Lacedemonians, because the Romans strove not only for magnanimity but directed all their actions to true justice. The type of happiness described above is that which we should seek the means of realizing or at least of approximating.

In seeking the realization of its mystic end, the State should be directed by laws both natural and divine. The underlying principle of direction will be that of harmony, which de l'Hôpital had recognized as the true essence of justice; the order of the State answering to that of the spiritual life and the well-governed family. Furthermore, inequality is of the essence of harmony, so that the good ruler like the good musician seeks an harmonic synthesis of many discordant elements, what Bodin calls an harmonic discord.[95] This idea naturally conducts our philosopher to views of relativity and reconciliation which, introduced into the *Methodus*, receive their application and fuller development in the *Republic*. He is led too to a defense of monarchy as an institutionalized order in obedience to the laws of God and Nature;[96] to an attack upon sixteenth century communism,[97] which sought, like certain modern theories, to obliterate rather than to harmonize distinctions of merit and corresponding inequalities of reward; and to an ideal of domestic order which, patterned after that of the mon-

---

[95] *République*, *VI*, Chapter 6. Compare Baudrillart, *op. cit.*, 155.

[96] *République*, *VI*, Chapter 4, 734 f.:—"Toutes les loix de nature nous guident à la monarchie: soit que nous regardons ce petit monde, qui n'a qu'un corps, et pour tous les membres un seul chef duquel depend la volonté, la mouvement, et sentiment: soit que nous prenons ce grand monde, qui n'a qu'un Dieu souverain: soit que nons dressons nos yeux au ciel, nous ne verrons qu'un soleil, et jusques aux animaux sociables, nous voyons qu'ils ne peuvent souffrir pleusieurs Roys, plusieurs seigneurs, pour bons qu'ils soient."

[97] *République*, Book I, Chapter 2, p. 11, and *Methodus*, Chapter VI. Compare de l'Hôpital, p. 27 above; and *Traité*, I, p. 112:—In the true republic, "les particuliers vivront mainteneus chascung selon leurs conditions, rangs et mérites en leurs biens, en leurs vies, leurs honneurs, eulx et leurs familles; qui est la fin et le but de l'intention de la justice."

archical state, reduced women to a subordinate position.[98] Finally, his principle of harmony leads him to an ideal of justice which is similar to that of de l'Hôpital and de la Noue in that admitting the claims of both tolerance and severity, it reflects the reason of the well-directed inner life and contributes to the realization of the well-ordered state. "Rien donc d'exclusif," writes Baudrillart, "dans la conception qu'il se forme de la République. Il est spiritualiste et positif, il s'attache à concilier Platon et Aristote, ou plutôt il est décidément en morale de l'école platonicienne, et en politique, il s'inspire de préference de l'esprit et de la méthode du philosophe Stagyrite. . . . La justice pour règle et pour objet de l'Etat; pour but de la société, la recherche des biens intellectuels et moraux et des biens matériels: ceux-la plus élevés, ceux-ci d'absolue nécessité, et devant etre assurés d'abord, tel est, en résumé, l'idéal de la politique aux yeux de Bodin. Il restera fidèle à ces inspirations de son début."[99]

At the centre of Bodin's speculative politic, compounded of Aristotelian and Platonic ideas, is his concept of sovereignty.[100] Without admitting the divine right of kings, Bodin argues for a permanent contract between the people, who are the true source of sovereignty, and the king. Sovereignty is absolute but it appears not inalienable; for the right of the king to dispose of his sovereignty as he would of his property is frankly admitted. Though it may be inherited as house and land, it may not be reclaimed by the people. In the use of his power, however, the king is not theoretically his own master. He is subject, according to our philosopher's synthesis of the spiritual, natural, and political life, to divine and natural laws. Should he violate these he is guilty of *lèse-majesté divine*. In his application of his theory of sovereignty to the practical business of the state Bodin seems to subtract something from the actual power which he had before assigned the Prince by denying him, for instance, the right to levy taxes upon the

---

[98] *République*, Book I, Chapter 3, *De la Puissance Maritale:*—"le commandement, qu'il [Dieu] avoit donné auparavant au mari par dessus la femme, porte double sens, et double commandement: l'un, qui est literal de la puissance maritale: et l'autre moral, qui est de l'ame sus le corps, de la raison sus la cupidité, que l'escriture saincte appelle quasi toujours femme, et principalement Salomon," etc., (p. 14).—"Mais quelque changement et varieté de loix qui puisse estre, il n'y a jamais eu loy ny coustume, qui ayt exempté la femme de l'obeissance, et non seulement de l'obeissance, ains aussi de la reverence qu'elle doit au mari, et telle que la loy ne permettoit pas à la femme d'appeler le mari en jugement sans permission du magistrat. Or tout ainsi qu'il n'y a rien plus grand en ce monde, comme dit Euripide, ny plus necessaire pour la conservation des Republiques, que l'obeissance de la femme au mari aussi le mari ne doit pas sous ombre de la puissance maritale, faire une esclave de sa femme" (p. 19).

[99] Baudrillart, *op. cit.*, 232.

[100] *République*, I, Chapters 8, 9, and 10. Compare Baudrillart, *op. cit.*, Chapter 6; and especially Hancke: *Bodin, Eine Studie über den Begriff der Souverainetät* in Heft 47 of Otto Gierke's *Untersuchungen zur Deutschen Staats- und Rechtsgeschichte*. Sidney Lee observes, *French Renaissance in England*, 321 f.: "It can hardly be questioned that Hooker derived from Bodin the doctrine of contractual sovereignty which was developed by Hobbes from the same source, and was afterwards admitted to the political creed of the English Whigs."

people at his pleasure. He fails to distinguish clearly, it would appear, between an absolute and a limited monarchy. The ideal of his political philosophy is, however, unmistakable, and it is of course that with which we are here concerned.

According to Bodin there are five marks by which sovereignty may be recognized. They are: first, the absolute power of legislating for all in general and for each in particular;[101] second the power of declaring war and peace;[102] third, the right of appointing the principal officers of the state;[103] fourth, the right of exercising the functions of the court of last appeal;[104] and fifth, the privilege of showing clemency.[105] In commenting upon the first of these marks of sovereignty, Bodin says that the prince in exercising his legislative powers should not be deterred by the customs of the country over which he rules. His dictum is: "La loi peut casser les coutumes, et la coutume ne peut deroger à la loi."[106] The magistrate "peut ployer la loy, et l'interpretation d'icelle, soit en douceur, soit en rigueur, pourveu qu'en la ployant il se garde bien de la casser."[107] Even the prince in exercising his privilege of clemency should remember his obligations to the laws of God and the interests of the state.[108] "La loi de Dieu dit qu'en punissant ceux qui ont merité la mort, ont osté la malediction d'entre le peuple; car de cent meschancetez il n'en vient pas deux en justice, et de celles qu'on y fait venir la moitié n'est pas verifiee; et si du crime verifié on ortroye grace, quelle punition pourra donc servir d'example aux meschants?"[109] As Baudrillart remarks:[110] "La sévérité ne déplait pas à Bodin. Il en parle avec approbation, avec amour. Pour lui, point de bon gouvernment sans un certain degré de rigueur. Il développe avec complaisance 'bien que la proposition, dit-il, puisse blesser les oreilles délicates' le proverbe: 'de méchant homme bon roi,' en ayant soin d'expliquer ce mot de méchant dans le sens de rigoureux." Equity, says Bodin, is not found "en douceur, contre la rigueur des loix;" equity "est de telle nature qu'elle n'a rien de commun avec la rigueur, ny avec la misericorde; mais elle resemble la reigle Lesbienne, laquelle estant de plomb, ploy aussi bien d'un costé que d'autre. Si le forfait est plus grand que les peines apposees aux loix ordinaires, le Magistrat qui cognoist extraordinairement doibt la peine; si la faute est moindre, il doibt adoulcir la peine, et non pas affecter le tiltre de Magistrat pitoyable, qui est l'un des vices à fuir autant, voire

[101] *République*, I, Chapter 10, 163.
[102] *Ibid.*, 164.
[103] *Ibid.*, 167.
[104] *Ibid.*, 169.
[105] *Ibid.*, 173.
[106] *Ibid.*, 162.
[107] *Ibid.*, 163.
[108] *Ibid.*, 175.
[109] *Ibid.*, 176.
[110] Baudrillart, *op. cit.*, 293

plus que la cruauté. Car la cruauté, bien qu' elle soit à blasmer, retient les sujets en l'obeissance des loi; et la trop grande doulceur, fait mespriser les Magistrats et les loi, et le Prince qui les a establies."[111] The proper temper for the magistrate he describes as a "gravité douce"; and those are to be blamed who in the execution of justice "se cholerent, menassent et injurient, ceux qu'ils jugent: comme faisoit ordinairement Claude l'Empereur, qui getta un jour le tranche-plume aux yeux de celuy qu'il jugeoit, avecques un visage plus bestial qu'Imperial."[112] But Bodin, like de l'Hôpital, looks beyond the picture of the grave judge administering the law with due dignity and severity to the end of all laws human and divine, which he declares is "d'entretenir l'amour entre les hommes et des hommes envers Dieu: ce qui ne se peut mieux faire, que par frequentation et union ordinaire."[113] "Paroles belles et précises," exclaims Baudrillart, "qui marquent dignement le rôle de la sociabilité et de la charité parmi les hommes, à côté, et en un certain sens audessus même de la justice? Si c'est la justice qui règle la société, c'est la sympathie qui la fonde, et c'est la charité qui la maintient "[114]

To the subject of sedition Bodin makes a particular application of his views of justice and mercy. "Si on voit qu'on ne puisse appaiser la faction par justice et jugemens, le souverain y doit employer la force, pour l'estaindre du tout, par la punition de quelquesuns des plus apparents; et mesmement des chefs de partie; et n'attendre pas qu'ils se soient tellement fortifiez, qu'on ne puisse leur faire teste."[115] So far as differences of religion are concerned one should proceed in a conciliatory spirit, turning hearts and wills to the true religion without violence or penalty; lest those who are frustrated in the exercise of their chosen religion should become atheists.[116] Nevertheless, "en matiere de seditions et tumultes, il n'y a rien plus dangereux que les sujets soient divisez en deux opinions, soit pour l'estat, soit pour la religion, soit pour les loix et coustumes; et au contraire, s'il s'en trouve de plusieurs opinions, les uns moyennent la paix, et accordent les autres, qui ne s'accorderoient jamais entr'eux."[117]

The subject of religious tolerance comes in for extended treatment in Bodin's *Heptaplomeres*, an imaginary dialogue in which the spokesmen of

[111] *République*, III, Chapter 5, 330 f.
[112] *Ibid.*, 331.
[113] *République*, III, Chapter 7, 349.
[114] Baudrillart, *op. cit.*, 327.
[115] *République*, IV, Chapter 6, 465.
[116] Baudrillart, *op. cit.*, 392.
[117] *République*, IV, Chapter 6, 478 f.—For this we find a classical parallel in the *Heptaplomeres* IV [216], 33: "Toralbe:—Il est vray que les sectes des Academiciens, des Stoiciens, des Peripateticiens, des Epicuriens, et des Cyniques disputoient l'une contre l'autre, cependant ils ne troubloient point l'union et la paix de la ville par ce que les Academiciens et les Peripateticiens estoient comme un milieu pour reunir les Epicuriens et les Stoiciens qui estoient entierement opposés. Autrement s'il ne se trouvoit quelque milieu pour rassembler les contraires il faudroit necessairement qu'il y eust partout une guerre perpetuelle."

many faiths, religious and philosophical, take part. The discussion, so far as it is conclusive, is in favor of tolerance and in praise of edicts which protect liberty of conscience. A further consideration of this interesting work[118] would take me too far afield; and I shall mention only in passing the *De Magorum Daemōnomania*,[119] which shows the mysticism of Bodin run to the seed of superstition; and the unenlightened scientific treatise that was entitled *Amphitheatrum Naturae*. The last two works serve only to make clear the limitations of a curious and adventurous mind. By force of reason and imagination Bodin attempted, like a true child of the Renascence, a reconciliation of science and religion, and believed that in the farther reaches of the mystic quest was to be found the abiding sanction of the true ethic and politic. If he seems to us now to have blindly supported a discredited ideal of the state, we should remember that it was from no low motive that he spoke and wrote; it was indeed for no other end than that reason and the will of God should prevail. From the ways of mere political expediency and intrigue, from the *politique matérialiste*, he turned to the uprightness of the individual life and the integrity of the family as the true bases of the state. And here it is that anxious watchers for the dawn of true democracy may join hands with this apologist of monarchical institutions in a common faith that the ark of political covenants shall be kept inviolate; that passion shall not depose reason in councils of state; and that in the words of Bodin himself, God shall be recognized as the "grand politique et gouverneur de tout le monde."

I have presented here in its ideal aspects a philosophy of justice and sovereignty that was unhappily often tainted with selfishness. Among the policists were those who deserved the reproach that the name of the party implies and to which Bacon alludes, the reproach that attaches to men who sacrifice principle to policy. Catherine de' Medici denominated them religious hermaphrodites; and I have no doubt that there were policists who, to adapt a phrase of Montaigne's, carried a candle for St. George in one hand and a candle for the dragon in the other. When, however, we have made full allowance for Machiavellian duplicity—for the enemies of *les politiques* called them Machiavellian—and for diversity of motive, we must recognize that there emerged from the speculations of this sixteenth century party of the middle an ideal body of doctrine which challenged at once the intelligence and the sincerity of the extremists.[120] It had to bear

---

[118] Chauviré in *Colloque de Jean Bodin*, Introduction, p. 3, says, "Sans conteste, à n'envisager que le mérite artistique, l'*Heptaplomeres* est le meilleur ouvrage de Jean Bodin." Another dialogue which is of interest in our investigation is Pasquier's *Pour-Parler du Prince*, in which against the arguments of l'Escolier, le Curial, and le Philosophe, le Politique contends that everything should be done to preserve the harmony of the State.

[119] See von Bezold, Jean: "Jean Bodin als Okkultist und Seine Démonomanie," *Historische Zeitschrift*, 105 (1910), 1 ff.; with additions in *Historische Zeitschrift*, 106 (1911), 438–439.

[120] See the passage quoted below, p. 69 f., from F. von Bezold's "Jean Bodin's Colloquium Heptaplomeres u.d. Atheismus des 16 Jahrhunderts", Erster Teil, *Historische Zeitschrift* (1914) 113, 308 ff.

the reproaches that the right and the left have always heaped upon the party of the centre, and to incur the distrust to which the spirit of compromise and reconciliation has ever been exposed. In the higher reaches of its thought, on the other hand, it attained to a knowledge of spiritual freedom which sharply challenged the claims of organized bigotry and oppression; and it opposed to all sixteenth century doctrines of force and efficiency—whether Calvinistic, Machiavellian, or Jesuitical—a gospel of reasonableness. For the religious temper of the policists is opposed at all points to wilfulness—to the wilful Prince of Machiavelli, to the wilful Pope of the Papists, and to the wilful God of Calvin. The watchwords of de l'Hôpital's *Traité* are Sovereignty, Order, Justice, Piety, Tolerance— ideas not in conflict but in harmony with one another; for freedom and tolerance are to be insured only by sovereignty—the sovereignty of reason in the province of the spirit, the sovereignty of the responsible prince in the province of the commonwealth. It is not clemency but cruelty, to borrow the thought of Cicero, to relax the severity of justice when sovereignty is attacked. The king, Bodin said, could pardon private wrongs; but he must exact stern punishment for all sins against that sovereignty of which he is the divinely appointed custodian.

CHAPTER III

Spenser and Les Politiques

It was, I think, in knowledge of and sympathy with the philosophy of sovereignty and justice that I have outlined above that Spenser wrote his *Book of Justice* and his prose tract on Ireland. That the Cambridge group of which our poet was a member was interested in political philosophy is clear from the work of Harvey and the correspondence of Sidney; and that Cambridge men in Spenser's day were enthusiastic students of Bodin's *Republic* in particular is proved by the following passage from the *Letter Book* of Harvey—"You cannot step into a scholars studye but (ten to one) you shall litely finde open ether Bodin de Republica or Le Royes Exposition upon Aristotles Politiques or sum other like Frenche or Italian Politique Discourses."[121] Moreover it is clear that Harvey took a very personal interest in Bodin, which was doubtless due in no small measure to the commendation which the French publicist, during his visit to Cambridge, had bestowed upon the English scholar. Indeed it is not unlikely that it is Harvey to whom Bodin alludes as the interpreter of the *Republic* at Cambridge. When in *Pierces Supererogation* Harvey opposes to the insults of Nashe the commendations of "worthy favorers," he associates with the names of Bird and Spenser that of Monsieur Bodin;[122] and elsewhere he says in allusion to Sidney, Bodin ("register of realmes happinesse, Which Italyes and Fraunces wonder is"), Hatcher, and others: "let these speake By their sweet Letters, which do best unfould Harvey's deserved praise."[123] Else-

---

[121] *Letter-Book of Gabriel Harvey*, Edited by E. J. L. Scott, Camden Society, 1884, p. 79. Compare Padelford, "The Political, Economic, and Social Views of Spenser," *Journal of English and Germanic Philology*, vol. 14, No. 3, p. 399. For Le Roy, see, A. Henri Becker, *Loys Le Roy de Coutances*, Paris, 1896. Machiavelli, Le Roy describes as "un autheur sans conscience et sans religion"; Becker, *op. cit.*, p. 193.

[122] "I speake not onely to Mr. Bird, M. Spencer, or Monsieur Bodin, whom he nothinge regardeth: (yet I would his owne learning or judgments were anye way matchable with the worst of the three) etc.; *The Works of Gabriel Harvey*, edited by A. B. Grosart, II, 83.

[123]   Sidney, sweet Cignet, pride of Thamesis;
   Apollos laurell ; Mars his proud prowess
   Bodine, register of Realmes happiness,
   Which Italyes, and Fraunces wonder is.
   (*Op. cit.*, II, 24.)

Compare:—

   Him whom thou raylest on at thine owne lust,
   Sith Bodine and Sweet Sidney did not flatter,
   His Invective thee too much grace affordes.
   (*Op. cit.*, II, 23.)

where he takes Scott, the author of the *Discovery of Witchcraft*, to task for not dealing "more courteously with Monsieur Bodin,"[124] mentions Bodin's views of the golden age,[125] adopts his concept of Harmonic Justice,[126] and agrees with him in declaring that "the differences of commonwealths or regiments requireth a difference of laws and orders."[127] May we not safely conclude that Spenser was well acquainted with the most distinguished political treatise of his time, seeing that it was in vogue among his fellow collegians and the work of an author particularly affected by his friend Harvey?

Nor is it unlikely that he was acquainted with the works of de l'Hôpital and de la Noue. It is not necessary for me to prove such knowledge, since my study (at least as far as these writers are concerned) is one in literary environment rather than in immediate literary sources. But it is worth while to note Harvey's praise of de la Noue and Sidney's acquaintance with him[128] and possibly with de l'Hôpital.[129] In *Pierces Supererogation* Harvey

---

> Some Tales to tell, would I a Chaucer were:
> Yet would I not even now an Homer be:
> Though Spencer me hath often Homer term'd:
> And Monsieur Bodine vow'd as much as he.
> (*Op. cit.*, I, 252.)

Nash in *Have With You to Saffron-Walden* (*Works*, ed. Mc Kerrow, III, 116) writes:—"For M. Bodines commendation of him, it is no more but this, one complementarie letter asketh another; and Gabriell first writing to him, and seeming to admire him and his workes, hee could doo no lesse in humanitie (being a Scholler) but returne him an answere in the like nature."

[124] *Pierces Supererogation*, p. 291. See, further, *ibid.*, p. 231: "And art such a witch for a cherne or a cheese-presse, as is not to be founde in the mallet of witches, or in *Monsieur Bodines Daemonomania.*"

[125] *Letter-Book*, p. 86.

[126] *Pierces Supererogation*, p. 183.

[127] *Pierces Supererogation*, p. 137.

[128] Note the following from *The Correspondence of Sir Philip Sidney and Hubert Languet*, ed. W. A. Bradley:—"The Prince of Orange and La Noue especially welcomed him [Sidney's brother]; and La Noue, who is full of courtesy, showed him every attention yesterday as long as we were in the citadel. Your letters gave great pleasure to La Noue and the Prince; both of them thanked me warmly for what I have done towards gaining them your good-will. I have no doubt they will show you in their letters how well pleased they are" (Letter 63, Languet to Sidney, p. 177).—"You need not fear the coming of Alençon into this country: if he comes at all, it will hardly be before autumn; and if you should follow the camp only for a few months, you would derive great advantage from it, especially if you should improve your acquaintance with La Noue" (Letter 68, Languet to Sidney, p. 187).

[129] Sidney's residence in Paris for three months in 1572 makes it altogether probable that he met the Chancellor of France. The English traveller, who seems to have begun during this visit his friendship for Walsingham, the English ambassador, was of course very much at home at the English embassy. See Wallace, *Life of Sir Philip Sidney*, p. 119: "He may also have met Michel de l'Hôpital (1505–1573), the Chancellor of France, regarding whom he afterwards expressed the opinion that France had 'never brought forth a more accomplished judgment

writes: "It were an impossible attempte, to do right unto the great Captaine, Monsier de la Noue, and the brave soldiour, the French king himself, two terrible thunderboltes of warre, and two impetuous whirlewinds of the Field: whose writinges are like their actions, resolute, effectuall, valiant, politique, vigorous, full of aery and fiery spirite, honourable, renowned wheresoever Valour hath a mouth, or Vertue a pen."[130] Writing to Sidney from Antwerp under date of November 14, 1579, Languet declares: "In la Noue many excellencies contend for preeminence, besides which he possesses such skill in the Art of War, that the Prince (the Prince of Orange) himself and all the men of understanding here consider him the pillar of their party. . . . The friendship and intimacy of these two men, of whom I speak thus highly, will be already prepared for you if you come hither. They both love you and esteem you greatly;"[131] and in a letter of the following January Languet speaks of the advantages that Sidney will derive from improving the acquaintance of de la Noue.[132]

Like the policists in France and the spokesmen of religious tolerance in England, Spenser was the champion of order.[133] Like them he believed that intemperance and injustice breed disorder. And over his thoughts of justice and mercy presided that faith in divine sovereignty that contemporary philosophers and poets fondly entertained. It was only under the prince, righteous, merciful, and just, that the order and peace of the commonwealth were insured. To insult sovereignty was to insult God and to open the way for all injustice, impiety, and intolerance. These political ideas of Spenser are of course only projections of his Aristotelian ethic: the Prince should rule his country as reason rules the soul, to the end that the harmony of the well-directed inner life should be realized in the body politic. For princes, Spenser and Bodin agree, hold their titles

---

more firmly builded upon virtue.'" Professor Wallace's quotation is from the *Apologie for Poetrie*. The following allusion to the Latin poems of de l'Hôpital is not without interest in this connection:—"Rasse des Noeux to Walsingham: My delay in writing has been because I was waiting to send you the Latin poems of the late Chancellor of l'Hôpital, which are not yet ready owing to the death of the President de Pibrac, his close friend, who had undertaken to collect them and have them printed. As soon as they are out, I will send them to you and my Lord Treasurer. You will enjoy them, for they are excellent." (*Calendar, Foreign*, 1584–1585, p. 134.) See, too, p. 537 of the same volume of the Calendar.

[130] *Works*, Ed. Grosart, II, 104.

[131] *The Correspondence of Philip Sidney and Hubert Languet*, edited by W. A. Bradley, Boston, 1912; p. 184.

[132] *Op. cit.*, p. 187.

[133] de l'Hôpital, *op. cit.*, I, 13: "Je dis donc que ce qui rend non seulement tous estats, républicques, citez, familles, mais encore chascung homme particulier heureux ou malheureux, sain ou malade, bon ou maulvais, sage ou fol, juste ou injuste, doué de bonnes ou maulvaises qualites et conditions, c'est l'ordre ou le désordre. Cette maxime est des plus certaines, et se vérifie généralement en tout ce qui se trouve en l'univers; et de faict, y a il chose au monde qui estant hors de son lieu, rang et situation naturelle, ne soit incontinent en inquiétude, tourment et vexation?"

under both the law of God and the law of Nature. "C'est une loy divine et naturelle," writes Bodin, "d'obeir aux edits et ordonnances de celuy à qui Dieu a donné la puissance sur nous" (p. 111); and "tous les loix de nature nous guident à la Monarchie: soit que nous prenons ce grand monde, qui n'a qu'un Dieu souverain; soit que nous dressons nos yeux au ciel, nous ne verrons qu'un Soleil, et jusques aux animaux sociables nous voyons qu'ils peuvent souffrir plusieurs Roys, plusieurs seigneurs, pour bons qu'ils soient" (734-735). Spenser says that princes—who, according to the above passages, derive their titles from God, and are as it were the gods of their kingdoms—God makes

>like himselfe in glorious sight,
>To sit in his owne seate, his cause to end,
>And rule his people right, as he doth recommend.
>(F.Q.,V., Pr. 10)

And that this sovereignty is in accord with Nature as well as with the will of God, Spenser allegorically sets forth in the Mutability cantos, where he represents both heavenly powers and earthly wights as appearing before Dame Nature "for triall of their Titles and best Rights" (F.Q., VII, VI, 36). At the conclusion of the session of Nature's Court, Jove is "confirmed in his imperiall see."

Spenser and Bodin[134] also agree in the opinion that the sovereignty of the Prince rests upon a contract of permanent validity. The argument in the *Veue* is that the Irish, having accepted and acknowledged Henry VIII. as their liege lord, are still bound by his laws:—

Eudoxus: What is this which you say? And is there any part of that realme or any nation therin, which have not yet bene subdued to the crowne of England? Did not the whole realme universally accept and acknowledge our late prince of famous memory, Henry the Eighth, for theyr only king and liedge lord?

Irenaeus: Yes, verely: in a parliament houlden in the time of Sir Antony Sent-Leger, then Lord Deputye, all the Irish lordes and principall men came in, and being by sure meanes wrought therunto, acknowledged King Henry for theyr soverayne lord, reserving yet (as some say) unto themselves all theyr owne former priviledges and segnioryes inviolate.

Eudoxus: Then by that acceptaunce of his sovereynty they also accepted of his lawes. Why then should any other lawes be now used amongest them? . . . But doe they not still acknowledge that submission?

[134] *République*, I, Chapter 8, p. 89: "Et d'autant que nous avons dit que Republique est un droict gouvernement de plusieurs familles, et de ce qui leur est commun, avec puissance souveraine, il est besoin d'esclarcir que signifie puissance souveraine. J'ay dit que ceste puissance est perpetuelle: par ce qu'il se peut qu'on donne puissance absoluë à un, ou plusieurs à certain temps, lequel expiré, ils ne sont plus rien que sugets: et tant qu'ils sont en puissance, ils ne se peuvent appeller Princes souverains, veu qu'ils ne sont que depositaires, et gardes de ceste puissance, jusques à ce qu'il plaise au peuple ou au Prince la revoquer;" *ibid.*, p. 90:—"Or la souveraineté n'est limitee, ny en puissance, ny en charge, ny à certain temps;" *ibid.*, p. 93:—"Poursuivons maintenant l'autre partie de nostre definition, et disons que signifient ces mots Puissance Absolue. Car le peuple, ou les seigneurs d'une Republique, peuvent donner purement, et simplement la puissance souveraine, et perpetuelle à quelqu'un, pour disposer des biens, des personnes, et de tout l'estat à son plaisir, et puis le laisser à qui il voudra, et tout ainsi que le proprietaire peut donner son bien purement," etc. Compare, Hancke, *Bodin, Eine Studie über den Begriff der Souverainetät*, Breslau, 1894, pp. 18-19.

Irenaeus: Now they doe not; for now the heyres and posteritye of them which yeelded the same are (as they say) either ignoraunt therof, or doe willfully denye or stedfastly disavowe it.

Eudoxus: How can they doe soe justly? Doth not the act of the parent, in any lawfull graunt or conveyaunce, bind the heyres for ever thereunto? Since then the auncestours of those that now live yeelded themselves then subjectes and liedgemen, shall it not tye their children to the same subjection?"[135]

While accepting this view of the permanent contract Irenaeus argues that nothing thereby was given to Henry VIII. which he did not hold before from his ancestors; "for all other absolute power of principalitye he had in himself before derived from many former Kinges, his famous progenitors and woorthy conquerours of that land. The which, sithence they first conquered and subdued unto them by force, what needeth afterward to enter into any such idle termes with them to be called theyr King, wheras it was in the power of the conquerour to take upon himself what title he will over the dominions conquered. For all is the conquerours, as Tully to Brutus sayth. Therfore (me seemes) insteede of so great and meritorious a service as they bost they performed to the King, in bringing all the Irish to acknowledge him for theyr Leige, they did great hurt unto his title, and have left a perpetuall gall in the myndes of that people whoe, before being absolutely bound to his obedience, are now tyed but with termes, wheras els both theyr lives, theyr landes, and theyr libertyes were in his free power to appoynt what tenures, what lawes, what conditions he would over them which were all his: against which there could be no rightfull resistaunce, or yf there were, he might, when he would, establish them with a stronge hand."[136]

Here Spenser apparently has in mind the authority of Bodin's *monarchie seigneuriale*, described in the following passages from the *Republic*:—
(1) "puisque le consentement de tous les peuples a voulu, que ce qui est acquis par bonne guerre, soit propre au vainqueur, et que les vaincus soient esclavès des vainqueurs, on ne peut dire que la Monarchie ainsi establie soit tyrannique: veu mesmes que nous lisons, que Jacob par son testament laissant a ses enfans une terre qu'il avoit acquise, dist qu'elle estoit sienne, par ce qu'il l'avoit acquise à la force de ses armes." (2) "Et ne doit pas la monarchie seigneuriale estre appellee tyrannie: car il n'est pas inconvenient, qu'un Prince Souverain, ayant vaincu de bonne et juste guerre ses ennemis, ne se face seigneur des biens et des personnes par le droict de guerre, gouvernant ses sujets comme esclaves, ainsi que le pere de famille est seigneur de ses esclaves et de leurs biens, et en dispose à son plaisir" (Book II, Chapter 2, p. 204). Moreover Bodin agrees with Irenaeus that the *monarchie seigneuriale* is more stable than that based upon contract, as will appear in the following passage: "Et la raison pourquoy la Monarchie seigneuriale est plus durable que les autres, est pour autant qu'elle est plus

---
[135] *Globe Spenser*, p. 611.
[136] *Globe Spenser*, p. 612 f.

auguste, et que les sugets ne tiennent la vie, la liberté, les biens (Spenser's "theyr lives, theyr landes, and theyr libertyes"), que du Prince souverain, qui les a conquestez à juste tiltre" (Book II, Chapter 2, p. 204).

To Spenser, as to de l'Hôpital and Bodin, justice like sovereignty derives from God. Princes, he says, have been endowed with this virtue by the divine grace; it is the most sacred virtue resembling God himself. The eye of the poet glancing from earth to heaven sees justice sitting highest in the seat of judgment, in the Almighty's stead. Gods and men equally adore it, and highest Jove dispensing justice to the inferior gods therewith contains his heavenly commonweal. The rôle of mercy in the execution of justice Spenser and the policists agree, is not that of a mere humanitarian virtue, making concessions to human weakness. In describing the character of Lord Grey, Spenser, as we have seen, had in mind that distinction between *clementia* and *misericordia* which is insisted upon by de l'Hôpital and Bodin; and just as de l'Hôpital declared that justice and mercy should never be separated, so Spenser says that they are like sun and moon—they both "like race in equall justice runne."

To the rôle of mercy in the dispensation of justice Spenser devotes two episodes of the fifth book of the *Faerie Queene*.[137] The first of these describes the visit of Britomart[138] to Isis Church on her way to the rescue of Artegall from Radigund. The virgin enters the temple with great humility;

[137] It is interesting to note that on the occasion of the Queen's visit to Audley End, Harvey took part in a disputation on the question, whether clemency or severity be more praiseworthy in a prince; see Morley, "Spenser's Hobbinol," *Fortnightly Review*, N. S., V, p. 277.

[138] Although it is Artegall who personifies Justice, his close association with Britomart suggests the classical personification of Justice as a beautiful virgin. This symbolism de l'Hôpital dwells upon in the *Traité*, opposing to his portrait of Justice another one of Injustice. The two allegorical figures correspond interestingly with the contrasted portraits of Radigund and Britomart in the *Faerie Queene:*—"Premièrement, parce qu'il n'y a rien qui fasse mieulx paroistre le contraire que l'opposant à son contraire: je dis que la justice est figurée fort proprement par Orphée, par Hésiode et aultres poëts anciens, en forme d'une vierge chaste et pudicque veneue du ciel, et fille de Jupiter, pour nous donner à entendre que la justice est ung don de Dieu mouvant immediatement de sa bonté, et mis en dépost comme chose précieuse et sacrée entre les mains des puissances terriennes pour la communiquer aux hommes mortelz, les faire vivre soubs la conduite et discipline d'icelle. . . . Chrysippe, mieulx que tout aultre d'entre les rhétoriciens, dépeint la justice fort élégamment. Filo videlicet ac forma virginali, adspectu vehementi ac formidabili, luminibus oculorum acribus, neque humilis, neque atrocis, sed reverendae cujusdam tristitiae dignitate. . . . A l'opposite d'elle il faut mettre l'injustice, et croire que c'est une fille volaige, impudicque, mensongère, bigarrée de toutes couleurs, et merveilleusement effrontée, sortie des enfers pour tourmenter et opprimer les innocents en ce monde, porter et favoriser les meschans, les combler pour ung temps des richesses acquises par rapine, par concutions, par tromperies, et leur donner toutes sortes d'advantaiges sur les gens de bien; et comme il n'y a rien si modeste, si affable que la vierge pudicque et bien apprise envers les bons et vertueux, si rude et si farouche et inaccessible à l'encoustredes impudens, luxurieux et desbordez, autant en est il de la justice. . . . Elle a véritablement le regard fort terrible et formidable, les yeulx pénetrants et perceants à la premiere renconstre, le port et contenance ny trop fier et relevé, ny trop simple et rabaissé, ains meslée d'une doulce et

but Talus, the iron man, who throughout represents the principle of stern executive justice, might not be admitted "to her part." The priests of Isis wear rich mitres shaped like the moon to show that Isis signifies the moon as Osiris does the sun: they both "like race in equal justice run." Having looked with wonder upon the stately building supported by goodly pillars "all diapred with shining gold," Britomart is brought to the Idol, cunningly fashioned in silver, clothed in garments of linen, and wearing upon her head a crown of gold to show that she has power in things divine. One foot of the goddess rests upon a crocodile and in her hand she holds a long, white, slender wand. The virgin knight prostrates herself in silent prayer before the image, and then perceiving that Isis with amiable countenance moves the wand, Britomart unlaces her helmet and lies down to sleep by the side of the altar. During the night there comes to her a wonderful vision. The white linen stole that she had assumed is suddenly turned to scarlet and her moon-like mitre to a crown of gold. Then there arises a great tempest that blows the holy fire and scatters the embers over the ground. At the moment when it seemed that the temple would be consumed by a conflagration, the crocodile opening his mouth devours both the flame and the tempest. Swollen with pride he is then about to devour the goddess herself, when with her wand she turns his pride to humility. He then sues for her love, she grants it, and of their union is born a lion of great might that quickly subdues all other beasts.

The following morning the gorgeous imagery of Britomart's dream is explained to her. The crocodile represents in the first instance Osiris and then the faithful lover of Britomart. His position under the foot of Isis shows that

> clemence oft, in things amis,
> Restraines those sterne behests and cruell doomes of his.

Moreover Britomart is told:

> That knight shall all the troublous stormes asswage,
> And raging flames, that many foes shall reare,
> To hinder thee from the just heritage
> Of thy sire's crowne, and from thy countrey deare.
> Then shalt thou take him to thy loved fere,
> And join in equall portion of thy realme:
> And afterwards a son to him shalt beare,
> That Lion-like shall shew his poure extreame.
> So blesse thee God, and give the joyaunce of thy dreame.

The second episode in the fifth book of the Faerie Queene which deals with the theme of mercy is that of Mercilla's House. Here Arthur and Artegall are led by Samient, whom the two knights have rescued from

---

affable aux bons, aux pauvres et affligez desquels elle est le reconfort: sa terreur, son épouvantable regard n'est que contre les meschans et les geans ou tyrans, ainsy que Plato, Cicéron, et l'Escriture mesme appellent ceux qui veulent résister aux efforts de la justice: Parcere subjectis, et debellare superbos.—*Op. cit.*, I, 68–69.

violence. Passing Awe, the warder of the castle, they find themselves in the midst of people making troublous din,

> as if that there were some
> Which unto them was dealing righteous doome.

In the midst of the crowd they encounter the marshal of the hall, whose name is Order. The clamor ceases as the people gaze upon the two knights;

> For never saw they there the like array;
> Ne ever was the name of warre there spoken,
> But joyous peace and quietness alway,
> Dealing just judgments, that mote not be broken
> For any brybes, or threates of any to be wroken.

Arthur and Artegall are guided to the queen Mercilla, who sits upon a throne adorned wih gems and "all embost with lyons and with flourdelice." Encompassing the throne were a thousand people singing hymns and carols. The queen holds in her royal hand a scepter which is

> The sacred pledge of peace and clemencie,
> With which High God had blest her happie land,
> Maugre so many foes which did withstand.
> But at her feet her sword was likewise layde,
> Whose long rest rusted the bright steely brand;
> Yet when as foes enforst, or friends sought ayde,
> She could it sternely draw, that all the world dismayde.

Attending upon the throne of Mercilla are just Dice, wise Eunomie, mild Eirene, and among them sit

> goodly Temperance in garments clene,
> And sacred Reverence, yborne of heavenly strene.

The knights are given seats on either side of Mercilla, while the trial of Duessa proceeds. Against the culprit appear Zeal, an old sage named the Kingdom's Care, Authority, the Law of Nations, Religion, the Commons, and Justice. Those who pleaded for her were Pity, Regard of Womanhood, Danger, Nobility of Birth, and Grief.

> Artegall, with constant firme intent,
> For zeale of justice was against her bent.

Mercilla, though hesitating for a time out of "piteous ruth," is at length constrained to enforce justice;

> And yet even then ruing her wilfull fall
> With more than needfull naturall remorse,
> And yeelding the last honour to her wretched corse.

> During all which, those knights continued there,
> Both doing and receiving courtesies
> Of that great ladie, who with goodly chere
> Them entertayn'd, fit for their dignities,
> Approving dayly to their noble eyes
> Royall examples of her mercies rare,
> And worthie paterns of her clemencies;
> Which till this day mongst many living are,
> Who them to their posterities doe still declare.

Passing from the House of Mercilla, Arthur proceeds against the Belgae, and Artegall goes to the rescue of Irena.[139]

There can be no mistake about the general significance of the Isis Church and Mercilla episodes. Grey is vowed heart and soul to the service of the Queen, who is at once merciful and militant. It is not simply that he owes allegiance to her, but that he loves those twin ideals of justice and mercy which, as the poet would have it, are the essence of her character and the inspiration of her life. In the person of Mercilla the merciful disposition of the Queen is further celebrated; and there is significance in representing Leicester and Grey as taking with them on their respective missions to the Netherlands and Ireland the lesson to be drawn from the trial of Mary Queen of Scots. That process has shown that the forces that make for order, justice, and peace (Eunomie, Dike, Eirene[139a])—in a word those that informed the nationalistic and eirenic policy of *les politiques*— were arrayed against the Catholic menace in the person of the Scottish queen; and Arthur and Artegall address themselves to their respective tasks with the example of the stern but sorrowful justice of Mercilla fresh in their minds. In Ireland, Spenser implies, Grey followed the example that the Queen had set in the execution of Mary and that was recommended to Leicester for his campaign in the Netherlands. Moreover, the association of the Scottish queen (the kinswoman of the Guises)[140] with Grey and Leicester in this episode stresses the international significance of Grey's mission to Ireland.

That Grey like the Queen was merciful as well as just Spenser declares in his poetry as he had done in his prose. More than once Artegall recalls Talus from the stern execution of justice.[141] For example, when the iron man sets upon the wild rout in Irena's kingdom,

---

[139] Grey, it will be remembered, was one of the commissioners appointed to try Mary, Queen of Scots, but this appointment came, as a matter of history, five years after his return from Ireland; *D. N. B.* VIII, 614.

[139a] Irena, too, may mean peace as well as Ireland; see Morley, *English Writers*, vol. IX, p. 394.

[140] The Duke of Guise is apparently alluded to in the following account of the family of Dolon (F. Q., V, 6, Stanza 33):—

> He had three sonnes, all three like fathers sonnes,
> Like treacherous, like full of fraud and guile,
> Of all that on this earthly compasse wonnes;
> The eldest of the which was slaine erewhile
> By Artegall, through his owne guilty wile:
> His name was Guizon; whose untimely fate
> For to avenge, full many treasons vile
> His father Dolon had deviz'd of late
> With these his wicked sons, and shewd his cankred hate.

As Innes says, *England Under the Tudors*, p. 310: "In England, Scotland, and Ireland the cause of Catholicism was the cause of Mary Stewart."

[141] The rôle of Talus in the administration of justice corresponds to that of force as described in the following passage from de l'Hôpital:—"Il fault donc, pour bien faire, joindre

> Artegall, him seeing so to rage,
> Will'd him to stay, and signe of truce did make:
> To which all harkning, did a while asswage
> Their forces furie, and their terror slake;
> Till he an herauld cald, and to him spake,
> Willing him wend unto the tyrant streight,
> And tell him that not for such slaughters sake
> He thether came, but for to trie the right
> Of fayre Irenaes cause with him in single fight.
>   (*F.Q.*, V, XII, St. 8.)

In applying his ideal of sovereignty and justice to the practical problems of the state Spenser came to conclusions similar to those which are expounded in the work of the policists. In agreement with Bodin (Book V, Chapter I) he argues that "lawes ought to be fashioned unto the manners and conditions of the people, to whom they are ment, and not to be imposed unto them according to the simple rule of right; for else (as I sayd) in steede of good they may worke ill, and pervert Justice to extreme Injustice."[142] Similarly Bodin:—"Il faut donc que le sage gouverneur d'un peuple scache bien l'humeur d'iceluy, et son naturel, auparavant que d'attenter chose quelconque au changement de l'estat ou des loix. Car l'un des plus grands, et peutestre le principal fondement des Republiques, est d'accommoder l'estat au naturel des citoyens, et les edits et ordonnances à la nature des lieux, des personnes, et du temps. Car quoy que die Balde, que la raison et l'equité naturelle n'est point bornee ny attachee aux lieux, cela reçoit distinction, c'est à scavoir, quand la raison est universelle, et non pas ou la raison particuliere des lieux et des personnes, reçoit une consideration particuliere" (p. 486).

Furthermore, Spenser and Bodin agree that those who have put themselves beyond the pale of the law cannot in justice appeal to it.

Iren. The Irish, in the violence of theyr furyes, treade downe and trample under foote all both divine and humane thinges, and the lawes themselves they doe specially rage upon, and rend in peeces, as most repugnant to theyr libertye and naturall freedome, which in theyr madnesse they affect.

Eudox. It is then a very unseasonable time to pleade lawe, when a swoord is drawen in the hand of the vulgar, or to thinke to retayne them with the feare of punishmentes, when they looke after libertye, and shake of all government.

Iren. Then soe it is with Ireland continually, Eudoxus; for the swoord was never yet out of theyr hand; but when they are weary of warres, and brought downe to extreeme wretchednes, then they creepe a little perhaps, and sue for grace, till they have gotten new

---

la force avec la justice, mais avec ceste différence que la force, comme le vassal, obéysse à la justice, comme à la dame de fief et maîtresse soubveraine, et ne face rien que soubs son authorité, vouloir et commandement."—*Traité*, 1, 88–89. Compare F. M. Padelford, "Talus, the Law," *Studies in Philology*, University of North Carolina, XV, No. 2, 97 ff.

[142] *Globe Spenser*, p. 613. Compare Harvey, *Pierces Supererogation*, (*Works* II, p. 137): "The difference of Commonwealthes, or regiments, requireth a difference of lawes, and orders: and those lawes, and orders are most soveraine, that are most agreable to the regiment, and best proportioned to the Commonwealth."

breath and recovered their strength agayne. Soe as it is in vayne to speake of planting of lawes, and plotting of pollicyes, till they are altogether subdued (p. 614).

"Des loix humaines," Bodin writes, "ont toujours separé les brigans et corsaires, d'avec ceux que nous disons droits ennemis en fait de guerre: qui maintiennent leurs estats et Republiques par voye de justice, de laquelle les brigans et corsaires cherchent l'eversion et ruine. C'est pourquoy ils ne doivent jouyr du droit de guerre commun à tous peuples, ny se prevaloir des loix que les vainqueurs donnent aux vaincus." (Book I, Chapter I, p. 1 f.)

In the next place Spenser's opinion of religious persecution should be compared with that of Bodin. Irenaeus blames the Roman Church for the sad spiritual state of the realm: "Litle have I to say of religion, both because the partes therof be not many, (it self being but one) and my self have not beene much conversaunte in that calling, but as lightly passing by I have seene or heard: Therfore the faulte which I finde in Religion is but one, but the same is universall throughe out all the countrey; that is, that they are all Papistes by theyre profession, but in the same soe blindely and brutishly enformed (for the most parte) as that you would rather thinke them Atheistes or Infidells," etc. (p. 645); but so far is he from approving religious persecution that he declares "instruction in religion needeth quiett times, and ere we seek to settle a sounde discipline in the clargye, we must purchase peace unto the layetye; for it is an ill time to preache amongest swoordes,[143] and most harde, or rather impossible, it is to settell a good opinion in the myndes of men for matters of religion doubtfull, which have a doutless evill opinion of ourselves; for ere the newe be brought in, the old must be removed" (p. 646). This opposition to religious persecution is expressed even more emphatically in a later passage:—"For religion litle have I to saye, my selfe being (as I sayd) not professed therein, and it selfe being but one, soe as there is but one waye therin; for that which is true onelye is, and the rest are not at all, yet in planting of religion thus much is needfull to be observed, that it be not sought forcebly to be impressed into them with terrour and sharpe penalties, as nowe is the manner, but rather delivered and intimated with mildeness and gentleness,[144] soe as it may not be hated afore it be understood, and theyr Professors dispised and rejected. For this I knowe that the most of the Irish are so far from understanding of the popish religion as they are of the protestauntes profession; and yet doe they hate it though

---

[143] See de la Noue, *Discours*, p.397: "En fin les choses passees ont demonstré que les Princes, qui par guerres ont voulu accompagner la vehemence des prestres, ont desfiguré leurs Estats, et diminué leur grandeur."

[144] Compare Harvey (*Works*, II, 141 f.): "Were none more scrupulous, then S. Paul, how easily, and gratiously might divers Confutations bee reconciled, that now rage, like Civill Warres? The chiefest matter in question, is no article of beliefe, but a point of pollicy, or governement: wherein a Judiciall Equity being duely observed, what letteth but the particular Lawes, Ordinances, Injunctions, and whole Manner of Jurisdictions, may rest in the disposi-

unknowen, even for the very hatred which they have of the English and theyr government. Therefore it is expedient that some discreete ministers of theyr owne countreymen be first sent amongest them, which by theyr milde persuasions and instructions, as also by theyr sober life and conversation, may drawe them first to understand, and afterwardes to embrace, the doctrine of theyr salvation" (p. 679).

Note the similarity of the above quotations to the following from the fourth book of Bodin's *Republic:*—"Je ne parle point icy laquelle des religions est la meilleure, (combien qu'il n'y a qu'une religion, une verité, une loy divine publiee par la bouche de Dieu) mais si le Prince, qui aura certaine asseurance de la vraye religion, veut y attirer ses sugets, divisez en sectes et factions, il ne faut pas à mon advis qu'il use de force, car plus la volonté des hommes est forcee plus elle est revesche: mais bien ensuivant et adherant à la vraye religion sans feinte ny dissimulation il tournera peut estre les cueurs et volontez des sugets à la sienne, sans violence, ny peine quelconque; en quoy faisant non seulement il evitera les emotions, troubles, et guerres civiles, ains aussi il acheminera les sugets devoyez au port de salut" (p. 478).

Furthermore, we might note the grounds upon which both Spenser and Bodin oppose the doctrine of communism. Bodin's idea of "harmonic discord" reappears unmistakably in Artegall's debate with the Giant (Book V, Canto II, Stanza 34 ff.); and that justice and the natural law justify the subordination of women to men is an opinion common to the English poet and the French publicist. It is perhaps worth while to place side by side the following passages from the *Faerie Queene* and the *Republic:*—

> Such is the crueltie of women kynd,
> When they have shaken off the shamefast band,
> With which wise Nature did them strongly bynd,
> T'obay the heasts of mans well-ruling hand,
> That then all rule and reason they withstand,
> To purchase a licentious libertie.
> But vertuous women wisely understand,
> That they were borne to base humilitie,
> Unlesse the heavens them lift to lawfull soveraintie.
>   (Book V, Canto V, Stanza 25.)

Before leaving the palace of Radigund Britomart changed
> all that forme of commonweale,
> The liberty of women did repeale,
> Which they had long usurpt: and them restoring
> To mens subjection, did true Justice deale:
> That all they, as a Goddesse her adoring,
> Her wisedome did admire, and hearkned to her loring.
>   (Book V, Canto VII., Stanza 42.)

---

tion of Soveraine Autoritie? Whose immediate, or mediate actes, are to be reverenced with Obedience, not countermanded with sedition, or controled with contention." The interest of Harvey's opinions to students of Spenser's "Puritanism" has already been remarked by Professor Tolman in *Modern Philology*, XV, 549 ff., "Spenser and Harvey and Puritanism."

Compare with these quotations the following from the Republic—"Il n'y a jamais eu loy ny coustume, qui ayt exempté la femme de l'obeissance, et non seulement de l'obeissance, ains aussi de la reverence qu'elle doit au mari" (*op. cit.*, p. 19); "il n'y a rien plus grand en ce monde, comme dit Euripide, ny plus necessaire pour la conservation des Republiques, que l'obeissance de la femme au mari;" (*op. cit.*, p. 19); "la loy de Dieu et la langue saincte, qui a nommé toutes choses selon sa vraye nature et proprieté appelle le mari Bahal, c'est à dire, le seigneur et maistre, pour monstrer qu'à luy appartient de commander. Aussi les loix de tous les peuples, pour abaisser le cueur des femmes, et faire cognoistre aux hommes, qu'ils doivent passer les femmes en sagesse et vertu, ont ordonné, que l'honneur et splendeur de la femme, dependroit du mari" (*op. cit.*, p. 20); "celles, qui prennent si grand plaisir à commander aux maris effeminez, ressemblent à ceux, qui ayment mieux guider les aveugles, que de suivre les sages et clairvoyans" (*op., cit.* p. 20).

Although Spenser preserves his poet's faith in the golden age, his method as an historian of the Irish people, their customs and laws is similar to that advocated by Bodin. His cautious use of historical sources reminds us of his French contemporary:—

Eudox. You doe very boldly, Irenaeus, adventure upon the historye of soe aunciont times, and leane to confidently unto those Irish Chronicles which are most fabulous and forged, in that out of them you dare take in hand to lay open the originall of such a nation soe antique, as that noe monument remayneth of her beginning and first inhabiting there; specially having bene in those times allwayes without letters, but onely bare traditions of times and remembraunces of Bardes, which use to forge and falsifye every thing as they list, to please or displease any man.

To this objection, Irenaeus replies that he has checked up the Bards by referring to other sources:—

Iren. Truly I must confess I doe soe, but yet not soe absolutely as you suppose. I doe herin relye upon those Bards or Irish Chroniclers, though the Irish themselves, through theyr ignoraunce in matters of learning and deepe judgement doe most constantly beleve and avouch them, but unto them besides I add my owne reading; and out of them both togither, with comparison of times, likewise of manners and customes, affinitye of woordes and names, propertyes of natures and uses, resemblances of rytes and ceremonyes, monumentes of churches and tombes, and many other like circumstaunces, I doe gather a likelihood of trueth; not certaynlie affirming anything, but by conferring of times, languages, monumentes, and such like, I doe hunte out a probabilitye of thinges, which I leave to your judgement to beleve or refuse. Nevertheless there be some very aunciont authors which make mention of these things, and some moderne, which by comparing them with present times, experience, and theyr owne reason, doe open a window of great light unto the rest that is yet unseene.[146]

It is then Bodin's *assensio probabilis* that Spenser recognizes in granting that he is merely "hunting out a probability of things"; and he endorses the Frenchman's philological method in such phrases as "affinitye of wordes and names" and "conferring of languages." Later he argues that the

[146] *Globe Spenser*, 625 f.

people of Spain in part derive from the Gauls by citing what he considers Gaulish proper names—such as *Rhegni, Presamarii, Tamariti,* etc. Elsewhere the poet's philological interest is shown by his inquiry into the meaning and derivation of such words as *coygnye* and *kincogish.* One might add that he shares Bodin's distrust of oral tradition, as appears in the following words of Irenaeus: "neither is there any certayne hold to be taken of any antiquitye which is receaved by tradition, since all men be lyars and may lye when they will"[146] (p. 626).

From what has been said it seems to me clear that Spenser's interpretation of Lord Grey's character, answering to the Roman type of the judge merciful in temper but stern in the execution of justice; that his account of the proper relations of justice and mercy; that his advocacy of religious tolerance attended by his loyalty to a single religion; that his attack upon communism with his defense of "harmonic discord" in things economic; that his appeal to the law of God and the law of Nature as sanctioning the sovereign power of the Prince—in general his *politique spiritualiste* as contrasted with the *politique matérialiste* of Machiavelli; that his belief in the permanence of the contract between king and people and in Sovereignty based upon conquest; that his opposition to "women's rights" in the sixteenth century;—that all of these ideas or judgments make interesting and significant points of contact between the thought of Spenser and the speculative and empiric politic of *les politiques.* Furthermore, it should appear that the *Veue* regarded as an historical treatise is in general

[146] One or two other parallels between Spenser and Bodin may be noted. Irenaeus says (p. 767): "By the lawes of all kingdomes it is a capitall crime to devise or purpose the death of the King: the reason is, for that when such a purpose is effected, it should then be too late to devise therof, and should turne that common-weale to more hurt by such loss of theyr Prince, then such punishment of the malefactours." Bodin says (Book IV, Chapter 7, p. 465) that the punishment of a small number of conspirators may keep the great body of subjects to their duty; "sans user de gesnes, et tortures, en cherchant ce qu'on ne voudroit pas trouver: aussi ne faut-il pas dissimuler si le coulpable est descouvert avoir conjuré contre la vie du souverain, ou mesme l'avoir voulu." "Noe lawes of man (according to the straight rule of right) are just," says Irenaeus, "but as in regard of the evills which they prevent, and the safety of the commonwealth which they provide for." Similarly Bodin in the *Methodus*, p. 9 writes:—"Jurisprudentia est ars tribuendi suum cuique, ad tuendam hominum societatem" (Compare Renz, *op. cit.*, p. 93). In connection with what is said in the *Veue* (pp. 791 and 830) about the activity of the Irish bards and priests in keeping alive sedition, and about the need of a wholesome activity on the part of the "Ministers of England" it might be worth while to call attention to Bodin's views in regard to the relation between eloquence and sedition in the Republic, Book IV, Chapter 7, p. 483:—"C'est donc un cousteau fort dangereux en la main d'un furieux homme, que l'eloquence en la bouche d'un harangueur mutin. Et neantmoins c'est un moyen à ceux qui en veulent bien user, de reduire les peuples de Barbarie à humanité, c'est le moyen de reformer les moeurs, corriger les loix, chastier les tyrans, bannir les vices, maintenir la vertu: et tout ainsi qu'on charme les aspics, les viperes, les serpens par certaines parolles, ainsi les Orateurs charment les plus sauvages, et cruels hommes par la douceur d'eloquence: comme disoit Platon. Et n'y a point de moyen plus grand d'apaiser les seditions et contenir les en l'obeissance des Princes, que d'avoir un sage et vertueux prescheur, par le moyen duquel on puisse fleschir et ployer doucement les cueurs des plus rebelles."

written in the scientific spirit which Bodin in advance of his age advocated. More particularly, Spenser's recognition of the unreliability of oral tradition; his emphasis upon the method of comparison and collation; his concession that the historian for all his care deals with probability, not certainty; his interest in the philological method of investigating racial origins; his acquaintance with the theory of milieu in what he calls the "genius of the soil" (p. 609); and his opinion in general that the laws of a people are important for an understanding of their history and racial characteristics bring his historical method into striking correspondence with that expounded and recommended in Bodin's *Methodus*.[147]

[147] It is perhaps worth noting that on at least one occasion English government was recommended to the Irish by another than Spenser with reference to principles expounded by Bodin. The French writer's concept of Harmonic Justice was extended in the last Chapter of the *Republic* to forms of the State: "Mais nous dirons en continuant que ce n'est pas assez de soustenir que la monarchie est le meilleur estat, et qui moins a d'incommoditez, si on ne dit Monarchie Royale: et ne suffist pas encores de dire que l'estat Royal est le plus excellent, si on ne monstre aussi qu'il doibt estre temperé par le gouvernement Aristocratique et populaire, c'est à dire par Justice harmonique, qui est composee de la justice distributive ou Geometrique, et commutative, on Arithmetique, lesquelles sont propres à l'estat Aristocratique, et Populaire." The idea of Harmonic Justice, the praise of Monarchy, the duty of the government to encourage virtue and suppress vice, the value of both clemency and severity are all dwelt upon in an oration delivered (May 14, 1586) by Justice Walshe, Speaker of the Commons in the Irish Parliament, during the deputyship of Sir John Perrot (*Calendar, Ireland*, 1586–1588, p. 55 ff.). The following passages are quoted from the oration: "Value of gratitude, Praise of Monarchy. If then the Kingly state be of all other the best, and that we see the same more firmly established with us at this present, then it hath been at any time since the conquest of this land, we have great cause to hope that we shall be imparted with the blessings which evermore do accompany the same. But when we shall see that the government of Her Majesty's laws does not only confirm that monarchy, but also that it draweth thereunto the best parts of the other two (aristocracy and democracy) to the universal comfort of all estates, what is there more of earthly felicity that can be required? In this Most High Court of Parliament are in meet proportion annexed the Sovereign Majesty of a Prince, the Honourable Assembly of Peers, as well of them whose wont is with sound persuasions to mollify men's minds, as also of others to whom, in God, their Prince and country's cause, no travail can seem loathsome or be too painful, and lastly a brotherly society of Commons, who are called to this Council as interested for the multitude, and hereby is wrought the most assurance that can be of holding the public wealth in that happy stay, when the Prince willeth only that is lawful, the Peers of all sorts have equal authority and none have voices but choice persons of the Commons. And herein is also seen a just poising of the three estates in such sort as the one seemeth to stand against the extremities of the other. . . . And where virtue is most exalted, and vice most suppressed, there are you to yield highest praise, and that (by the opinion of Mr. Fortescue; as Fortescue, sometime Lord Chancellor of England, writeth in his book, entitled, De laudibus legum Angliae) is performed by this governement. And where the transgressors of law are punished most to the satisfaction of all men, and without opinion of cruelty, there least inconvenience will ensue that justice. And as Cicero said that the laws of the 12 tables did more direct men to live well than did all the works of the philosophers, so may I say by our laws that they do little less draw men to virtue and withdraw them from vice than do the persuasions of preachers; for that alas! Man's frailty is such, that the greater number will be sooner moved by the allurements and terrors of this world than by that is to be expected

It was then an ideal of sovereignty and justice which was familiar to Englishmen and which had received particular attention in the speculative politic of contemporary France that Spenser brought to bear upon his defense of Lord Grey. In the spirit of the policists he regarded the seditions and insurrections of the Irish chieftains and the Irish priests as capital offenses against the peace of a divinely ordered world, whose natural course was to the end that reason and the will of God should prevail. The rebels should be punished with severity, for *severitas* as distinguished from *crudelitas* was essential to justice. But lest Lord Grey should be charged with the vice of *crudelitas*, Spenser takes pains to remind us that severity is not inconsistent with *clementia* as distinguished from *misericordia*, and that the English deputy was never guilty of that atrocity of the mind which Seneca marks as the true antithesis of clemency. His business was a stern one but his heart was never hardened.[148]

This portrait of the righteous judge, dealing strict justice more in sorrow than in anger, the guardian under sovereignty of the ordered peace of the world, is to be found not only in the work of the French policists but in the championship by Bacon and the Anglican apologists of the twin ideals of political sovereignty and religious tolerance. These ideals, based as we have seen upon a political philosophy compounded of Platonism, Aristotelianism, and Christianity, were manifestly congenial with the philosophy of the *Faerie Queene*. In availing himself of the wisdom of the ancient world to which as a humanist he had fallen heir, in recognizing the kinship of Christ and Plato, which Ficino commemorated when he lit his twin tapers before the crucifix and the bust of the Greek philosopher, Spenser put himself in the spirit of a new reformation which tried to be as true to the teachings of humanism as it was to the precepts of Christ—the reformation of justice and tolerance arrayed against misrule and persecution whether Protestant or Catholic. It was a reformation to which as we have seen the scepticism of Montaigne paid its respects and to which Bacon and Hooker made substantial contribution. Its polity and philosophy were enlisted in the cause of nationalism in both England and France, and its institutional expression and embodiment we might recognize in the Church of England. Its mind was the mind of Richard Hooker and its spirit was the spirit of Shakespeare.

---

in the world to come, and when some be (by this means) brought to the love of virtue, and vice is made hateful to them, then are they easily formed to the frame whereunto preachers desire to bring them. . . . It may not be denied but that Her Majesty hath with far more clemency than was to be expected by us, respited multitudes of them whom Her Highness's justice was to condemn, for as God gave her success over her rebellious subjects, so the fury of the rebellion being pacified Her Majesty was no less desirous to preserve her people than Scipio Africanus Major was to defend his Romans."

[148] Bodin says of Augustus, *République* III, Chapter 5, 331:—"Auguste faisoit bien autrement, car combien qu'il fust estimé fort entier, en droict en Justice, si est-ce qu'il ne condamnoit jamais à mort qu'en souspirant, comme dit Seneque."

CHAPTER IV

SPENSER AND MACHIAVELLI

I might here bring my study to a close were it not that Professor Greenlaw published several years ago in Modern Philology[149] an explanation of Spenser's defense of Lord Grey which is fundamentally different from mine. It is his opinion that the *Veue of the Present State of Ireland* defends the Lord Deputy's administration of Irish affairs according to the principles and precepts of the Machiavellian politic. That Machiavelli was an influence in and out of England during the sixteenth century no one would deny; but that Spenser, even though we credit him with a more intelligent understanding of Machiavelli than was common in his time, defended Lord Grey as an accomplished Machiavellian seems to me in the light of the idealism of the *Faerie Queene* a very doubtful contention. Furthermore, I hope that the preceding pages have made clear that the English poet was in sympathetic contact with a body of political speculation that was openly antagonistic to Machiavelli.

To support his contention that the *Veue* has "the distinction in Elizabethan literature of rightly interpreting Machiavellism," Professor Greenlaw argues that "in its general scheme, the *Veue* follows *Il Principe* very closely;" that the second division of the *Veue* shows "most directly the debt to Machiavelli;" that there are significant verbal parallels, similarities in structure and style, and a direct reference to Machiavelli with an illustration drawn from the *Discorsi*, besides other indications that Spenser knew this particular work; and that Spenser acknowledges that his plan is not original with him. Besides these arguments are to be noted the Machiavellian tactics of Elizabethan statesmen and what may of course be taken for granted, Spenser's knowledge of Machiavelli.[150]

---

[149] *Modern Philology*, VII, 187 ff.

[150] The "Italian's popularity with the young English students" is another matter. That his work should be well known and frequently discussed was in the nature of things. In this sense we might say that Bernhardi has been popular in similar circles during the last few years. That, on the other hand, his political doctrine was approved by Harvey, Sidney, or Spenser I cannot believe. The allusions to Machiavelli quoted by Mr. Greenlaw from Meyer's monograph (Litterarhistorische Forschungen I), when read in their context, appear to be wholly playful in spirit. Sidney writes, "I never could be induced to believe that Machiavelli was right about avoiding an excess of clemency, until I learned from my own experience what he has endeavoured with many arguments to prove. For I, with my usual vice of mercy, endured at your hands not only injustice, but blows and wounds; hoping that such gentleness would at last bend the most hardened obstinacy. But I am disappointed in my hopes, and seeing that my remedy, far from diminishing, even increases the malady, I shall use it no longer, but I shall substitute wholesome severity for this empty show (for so in truth it is) of clemency"

It is certainly misleading to say that "in its general scheme the *Veue* follows *Il Principe* very closely." Of *Il Principe* there are three main divisions, the first dealing with a classification of principalities and rules for winning and maintaining them (Chapters I–IX); the second, with an attack on the mercenary system (Chapters XII–XIV); the third with rules that should govern the conduct of the Prince (Chapters XV–XXV); the last chapter (XXLV) being in the nature of a peroration. The *Veue*, on the other hand, is in the main given to an examination of the social and political evils in Ireland under the main headings of (a) the laws, (b) the customs, and (c) the religion of the country. Although these are topics which Machiavelli considered in the third chapter of the *Prince*, the general scheme of the Italian's work is quite different from that which Spenser has followed. Machiavelli classifies kinds of governments; Spenser, the evils of Ireland. Nor can we attach much importance to what Professor Greenlaw calls Spenser's text—Machiavelli's "Ma quando si acquistano stati in una provincia disforme di lingua, di costumi et d'ordini, qui sono le difficulta, a qui bisogna avere gran fortuna e grande industria a tenerli." This may be paralleled particularly in the first chapter of the fifth book of Bodin's *Republic*, the topical heading of which is *Du Reiglement qu'il faut tenir pour accommoder la forme de Republique à la diversité des hommes et le moyen de cognoistre le naturel des peuples.* Spenser's "ripping up of ancient histories," which Mr. Greenlaw considers reminiscent of Machiavelli, was the method usually pursued in political writings of the time, conspicuously so in Bodin's *Republic*.[151] And in this connection attention might be drawn to the conventionality in sixteenth century treatises on politics of the figure which compares the ruler to a physician and his acts and laws to remedies,—a figure which appearing in both

---

(Sidney to Languet, April 29, 1574; Bradley, *op. cit.*, p. 60). To this Languet replies, May 13, 1574 (Bradley, 69 f.):—"I admire the candour with which you warn me to beware of you, for that is the meaning of your fierce threats. But there you do not follow the advice of your friend Machiavelli, unless, perhaps, it is fear that has extorted those big and sounding words, and you thought that so I might be deterred from my intentions." As for Harvey we may note the following: "Ferraria could scarcely brooke Manardus, a poysonous Physitian: Mantua hardly beare Pomponatius, a poysonous Philosopher: Florence more hardly tollerate Macchiavell, a poysonous politican: Venice most hardly endure Arretine, a poysonous ribald: had they lived in absolute Monarchies, they would have seemed utterly insupportable" (Works, II, 94). And again in criticism of Nashe: "It was nothing with him to Temporise *in genere* or *in specie*, according to Macchiavels grounde of fortunate successe in the world; that could so formally, and featly Personise *in individuo* (Works, II, 299). Nashe in *Have With You to Saffron Walden* (Works, II, 137) quotes Harvey as calling Perne, "an apostate, an hipocryte, a Machiavill, a cousner, a jugler, a letcher."

[151] See Bodin's *Methodus, Cap. tertium, De locis historiarum recte instituendis*, pp. 30, 31:— "Quod igitur viri docti facere solent in aliis artibus, ut memoriae consulant, idem quoque in historia faciendum judico: id est, ut loci communes rerum memorabilium certo quodam ordine componantur, ut ex iis, velut e thesauris, ad actiones dirigendas exemplorum varietatem proferamus." Compare Robert Flint, *Historical Philosophy in France*, pp. 193, 195.

Spenser and Machiavelli Mr. Greenlaw regards as evidence of Machiavellian influence.[152] Nor when we remember that almost everybody quoted Machiavelli to his purpose, need we suppose that Spenser's approval of Machiavelli's opinion in regard to the power that should be delegated to governors gives support to the theory that the English poet approved in principal the Machiavellian politic.

The parallels which Mr. Greenlaw draws between the second division of the *Veue* and the first fourteen chapters of the Prince are in my judgment inconclusive because nearly all, if not all, the passages in question may be paralleled also in Bodin's *Republic;* because in some cases the similarity between Spenser and Machiavelli is not close enough to be significant; and because in still other cases the passages should be related to actual conditions in Ireland and to the military policy that was natural in the circumstances.

The first of Mr. Greenlaw's parallels I have already dealt with. The second pertaining to the necessity for strong remedies may be extended to Bodin's *Republic;* see above, page 44. Furthermore, Spenser needed no literary source for this detail of policy; he was simply approving the practise of the government. We may cite, for example, Sentleger to the Queen (*State Papers, Ireland,* 1574–1585 Preface, p. 85): "In this government it is thought good policy to make waste the five counties within this province, the corporate towns only excepted, holding it the only means to subdue and famish the traitors." For the need of promptness, which is to be sure

---

[152] De l'Hôpital, *Traité*, I, 350:—"Le mesme judgment se faict des officiers d'une ville, qui sont les vrays médecins du corps politique;" and *ibid.*, I, 15:—"Fault aussy par fois faire comme le bon chirurgien, qui veult crever ung apostume," etc. Further, D'Aubigné, *Histoire Universelle*, VIII, p. 25:—"Mais les cris des princesses de la Ligue tindrent bien leur partie à faire mettre aux Parisiens l'enseigne au vent contre le roi, qui apporta de foibles remèdes à si forte maladie;" Bodin, *Republique*, IV, Chapter 6, p. 463:—"Premierement nous poserons ceste maxime, que les factions, et partialitez sont dangereuses, et pernicieuses en toute sorte de Republique, et qu'il faut s'il est possible les prevenir par bon conseil: et si on n'y a pourveu auparavant qu'elles soient formees, qu'on cherche les moyens de les guarir: ou pour le moins employer tous les remedes convenables pour adoulcir la maladie;" *ibid.*, p. 481:—"Mais tout ainsi que le bon medecin previent les maladies, et s'il advient qu'une partie soit affligee soudainement d'une douleur violente, il appaise le mal present: et cela fait il applique les remedes aux causes de la maladie: aussi le sage Prince doit prevenir tant qu'il luy est possible les seditions, et quand elles sont advenues, les appaiser à quelque prix que ce soit: et puis voir les causes des maladies plus esloignees des effects, et y appliquer les remedes couvenables;" *ibid.*, Book IV, Chapter 3, p. 418:—"Et tout ainis que les plus sçavans Medecins aux accés les plus violents si les symptomes sont bons, ont plus d'esperance de la santé, que si l'accés est doux et languide: et au contraire, quand ils voyent l'homme au plus haut degre de santé qui peut estre, alors ils sont en plus grande crainte, qu'il ne tombe en extreme maladie, comme disoit Hippocrate: aussi le sage Politique voyant sa Republique travaille de tous costez, et presque accablee des ennemis, si d'ailleurs il apperçoit que les sages tiennent le gouvernail, que les sugets obeissent aux magistrats, et les magistrats aux loix, alors il prend courage, et promet bonne issue," etc.; *ibid.*, Book IV, Chapter 3, p. 419:—"Et jamais ne faut essayer *les remedes violents,* si la maladie n'est extreme, et qu'il n'y ait plus d'esperance."

in the case of such a situation as existed in Ireland a very obvious need, and which is harped upon in the dispatches, we may compare the following from the Republic: "Si une fois l'estincelle du feu de sedition est soufflee d'un vent impetueux, on n'y viendra jamais à temps. A quoi les gouverneurs et magistrats doivent tenir la main" (p. 467). Compare above, p. 45. Then Bodin agrees with Spenser and Machiavelli that "the imputation of cruelty is not to be feared" (see above, pp. 44 and 45), and that sharp punishment should be visited upon "the heades and principalls of any mischievous practize or rebellion," as appears in the following passage from the *Republic* (Book 4, Chapter 6, p. 465):—"Et si on voit qu'on ne puisse appaiser la faction par justice, et jugemens, le souverain y doit employer la force, pour l'estaindre du tout, par la punitione de quelques uns des plus apparents: et mesmement des chefs de partie: et n'attendre pas qu'ils se soient tellement fortifiez, qu'on ne puisse leur faire teste." In this connection one might compare a passage from Andrew Trollope's letter to Walsyngham (1581), (*State Papers, Ireland*, 1574–1585, Preface, p. 84):—"Every chief rebel's pardon is a hundred men's deaths." Compare further p. 45 above. For the idea of dispersing rebels and depriving them of their arms, Professor Greenlaw presents from the *Prince* the following parallel: "E per cosa si faccia o si provvegga, se non si disuniscono o dissipano gli abitatori, non si dimentica quel nome ne quelli ordini, ma subito in ogni accidente vi si ricorre (cap. v)." Here nothing is said about disarming, which is specifically mentioned in the following passage from the *Republic* (Book IV, Chapter 6, p. 480): "L'autre moyen est aussi d'oster les armes si on craint la sedition, qui est le plus ordinaire." As a parallel to the observation that "particular care must be taken to discipline the chiefs or nobles thoroughly," see the passage quoted earlier in this paragraph. For the plan of establishing colonies or plantations in Ireland, history not Italian literature furnishes the immediate source. If we need an historical citation, it might be furnished by Henry Wallop's letter to Walsyngham (*State Papers, Ireland*, 1574–1585, Preface, p. 82), where the suggestion is made that the Irish should be put to the sword and colonists sent in their place. The need of caution in introducing new laws for the Irish is an easy inference from Bodin's general principle that new laws should be accommodated to the nature of the people to whom they apply.[153] Here Machiavelli's suggestion does not agree with Spenser's. The former recommends as one of three possible courses that the people be permitted to live under their own laws; the latter makes the rather obvious remark that it is not "convenient to change all the lawes and make newe." Spen-

---

[153] See, too, Smith, *De Republica Anglorum*, p. 13:—"Certaine it is that it is always a doubtful and hasardous matter to meddle with the chaunging of the lawes and government which a man doth finde alreadie established." The passage is quoted in Professor Padelford's suggestive article, "The Political, Economic, and Social Views of Spenser," *Journal of English and Germanic Philology*, XIII, No. 3, p. 401.

ser's view is less in accord with that cited by Professor Greenlaw from Machiavelli than it is with the opinion of Bodin expressed in the third chapter of the fourth book of the *Republic,* which bears the title, *Que les changemens des republiques et des loix, ne se doivent faire tout à coup.* From this chapter I might quote the following (p. 49): "Et jamais ne font essayer les remedes violents, si la maladie n'est extreme, et qu'il n'y ait plus d'esperance. Ceste maxime a lieu en toute Republique, non seulement pour le changement de l'estat, ains aussi pour le changement des loix, des meurs, des coustumes: à quoi plusieurs n'ayans pris garde, ont ruiné de belles et grandes Republiques, soubs l'apast d'une bonne ordonnance qu'ils avoient empruntee d'une Republique du tout contraire à la leur: . . . la loy pour bonne qu'elle soit, ne vaut rien, si elle porte un mepris de soy-mesme: et au contraire la reverence de l'antiquité est si grande, qu'elle donne assez de force à la loy, pour se faire obeir de soy-mesmes sans Magistrats: au lieu que les edicts nouveaux, avec les peines y apposees, et tout le debvoir des officiers ne se peuvent entretenir, sinon avec bien grande difficulté: de sorte que le fruict qu'on doibt recueillir d'un nouvel edit, n'est pas si grand que le dommage que tire apres soy le mepris des autres loix, pour la nouveauté d'une." One should read the whole chapter, because I have space here to quote only a short passage from a lengthy discussion of the matter.

It should be noted in the case just cited as in others, that much more space is given by Bodin than by Machiavelli to the point under consideration. For example, the fortification of towns, Mr. Greenlaw's last point of comparison with the *Prince,* is a subject recognized in the title of the fifth chapter of the fifth book of the Republic: *S'il est bon d'armer, et aguerrir les sugets, fortifier les villes, et entretenir la guerre.* I refer particularly to the passage on p. 583ff. which bears the marginal title, *Les inconveniens de n'avoir point de forteresse.* Referring to the defeat of Richard III, by Richmond, Bodin remarks on page 585: "ce qui n'est point advenu es pays fortifiez, ou il y a lieu de retraicte, pendant qu'on rallie les forces." After "ripping up of ancient historyes" he concludes: "Voila les raisons, qui peuvent servir pour monstrer, qu'il est besoin de fortifier les villes." Once more the point is considered at such length that it must have impressed itself upon the mind of any reader of the *Republic.* Nevertheless it might be well to glance again at the *Calendar of Irish Papers* for a possible Celtic source to compete with the French and Italian claimants. That English soldiers needed no publicist to teach them the value of fortified places, the following might remind us (Nicholas Malbie to Burleigh, 8 April, 1880; *State Papers, Ireland,* 1574–1585, Preface, p. 63): "This day I took order that the abbey of Buresowle aforesaid should be fortified and strengthened, and that all the castles of the country standing upon straits, should be warded and kept for her majesty, etc. . . . Mc Williams also, and his brother Richard McOlyverus Boork and the chief gentlemen of the country, having considered the great benefit and commodity which might grow to the whole country, if a walled town were built and erected at Bures, made humble request, etc." Finally the single parallel cited by Professor Greenlaw from the *Discorsi*, pertaining to a grant of greater power to the deputy, can have little weight in the light of the standing complaints against the government and the Queen for their interference with the Irish campaigns.

I find it hard, too, to agree with Professor Greenlaw when he detects in the following passage an allusion to the *Principe:*—"I doe not thinke it convenient, though nowe it be in the power of the Prince, to change all the lawes and make newe, for that should breed a greate trouble and confusion." Surely we do not have to seek very far to find "Prince" used in the sense of sovereign even when the ruler is a woman. For example, in a letter from the Lords Justices to Walsyngham (*State Papers, Ireland*, 1574-1585, Preface p. 20) there is the following passage:—"We received letters from Turlough Lynagh in very good and dutiful terms, and withal another from his wife, which they inclose. She protests against 'quidam susurriones (qui) vobis exposuerunt quod transivi in Scotiam, causa adducendi Scotos et extraneos contra *Majestatem Principis.*'" Again in the *Calendar of Irish Papers*, 1574-1585, p. 55:—"An oration pronounced by Justice Walshe, speaker of the Commons in the Irish Parliament at the dissolving therof. Value of Gratitude. Praise of Monarchy. . . . In this most High Court of Parliament are in meet proportion annexed the Sovereign Majesty of a Prince, the honourable Assembly of Peers, as well of them whose wont is with sound persuasion to mollify men's minds, as also of others to whom, in God, their Prince and country's cause, no travail can seem loathsome or be too painful" etc.

In criticizing Professor Greenlaw's theory, we should recognize that he is not the first to interpret the sixteenth century *politique spiritualiste* as Machiavellian. Sixteenth century Jesuits had done the same thing. Petrus Ribadeneira in his *Princeps Christianus* (1595) classified as disciples of Machiavelli those "politici, qui solo nominis Christiani obtentu Christum acriter insectantur;" and declared that although even heretics confessed some religion, "Politici et Machiavelli sectatores nullam religionem agnoscunt, verae falsaeque delectum ac discrimen tollunt, eam duntaxat probantes, quam politico statui utilem judicarint. Religionem igitur haeretici ex parte, Politici omnino respuunt.—Nomine specieque exteriori catholicos ementiente, radicitus evulsam funditusque eversam catholicam fidem volunt."[154] F. von Bezold has explained so well the general situation with which we are here dealing that we may profitably quote him at length:—"In dieser seltsam gemischten Atmosphäre von Weihrauch und Blutgeruch, von ästhetischen Duften und okkultistischer

---

[154] Quoted by F. v. Bezold, "Jean Bodins Colloquium" etc., *Historische Zeitschrift*, 113, p. 308, Note 2.

Narkose, von Frivolität und Wissbegier, mussten wie von selbst "epikureische" oder "atheistische" Stimmungen Keime und Blüten treiben. Es bildete sich sozusagen ein Typus des Hofatheisten aus. Daneben und sehr oft, aber nicht immer im Zusammenhang mit dieser weltmännischen Denkmode griff gerade in Frankreich unter dem Eindruck der Religionskriege der "Politicismus" um sich, der mit seiner Unterordnung der Religion unter das Staatsinteresse von manchem Strenggläubigen für die allerfährlichste Schule der Gottesleugnung angesehen wurde. Mehr und mehr erhielt dabei Machiavelli als der wahre "Furst des Atheismus" den Vortritt. Aber man scheute sich nicht, auch Männer, wie den Kanzler L'Hôpital oder Bodin, deren ernster Patriotismus mit der verrufenen italienischen Gewissenlosigkeit nichts zu tun hatte, wegen ihrer Befürwortung der Toleranz mit dem gleichen Stempel zu versehen."[155]

If at this point we raise the question of Bodin's sources, we may freely concede, on the basis of the evidence that Chauviré has offered, that in many of the particulars noted and in others that do not come into consideration here the French publicist drew upon the works of Machiavelli, even though he nowhere acknowledges indebtedness to him. The *Republic* shows very prettily how a sixteenth century writer might incur large debts in the works of Machiavelli without winning "the distinction of rightly interpreting Machiavellism." Indeed on the basis of parallel passages Professor Greenlaw will find Bodin far more Machiavellian than Spenser. It is not only that in matters concerning the art of war and the conduct of government he naturally turned to the works of the great Italian; but he clearly shares with him a fully developed scientific interest in the state. However, over all that is empirical and practical in Bodin (and this element is large and important) there preside his piety and mysticism; so that he borrows not only from Aristotle and Machiavelli but from Plato, and Sir Thomas More, and de l'Hôpital. His genius, like that of Spenser, is eclectic; but like Spenser, too, he subordinates his practical politic to the higher claims of morality and religion. And for our special problem here we should emphasise not only that we find in Bodin the blend of mysticism and practical politics that the *Veue* and the *Legend of Justice* conjointly present, but that almost every, if not quite every, particular in Spenser that suggests Machiavelli may be found in the work of the openly and violently anti-Machiavellian Frenchman.

It is clear, I think, that any contoversalist can quote Machiavelli to his purpose. This was true in the sixteenth century and it is true in the twentieth. We find in the comprehensive work of the Italian the most edifying as well as the most cynical precepts. Besides, his strictures upon Catholic oppression, his recognition of the value of religion to the state, and his concern in many ways for the preservation of the commonwealth establish points of surface contact between his work and that of the French

[155] *Historische Zeitschrift*, Vol. 113, p. 308.

policists. It is not however in the recognition of such correspondences that we shall understand the relation between the champions of *realpolitik* and the exponents of the divinely ordered state. The difference is not in the material of their discourses but in their inspiration, their *weltanschauung*, in the emphasis and direction of their thought. Machiavelli reckons Moses with Cyrus, Romulus, and Theseus among those who by their courage and ability, and not by fortune, have risen to the rank of rulers, but he says "we may not discuss Moses, who was a mere executor of things ordained by God, yet he merits our admiration, if only for that grace which made him worthy to hold direct communion with the Almighty."[156] On the other hand, Hooker, de la Noue, and de l'Hôpital[157] by preference turned for guidance to the heroes of Old Testament story; and Bodin sanctified his shrewd and practical politic with a genuine piety and mysticism. Unlike the policists Machiavelli found the source of successful government in the self-reliant and organized valor of the prince, not in the divine law and the guiding hand of God. For Spenser and the policists the foundation of the state was virtue; for Machiavelli it was *virtu*.[158]

> Virtu contro al furore
> Prendera l'arme, e fia il combatter corto;
> Che l'antico valore
> Negli Italici cuor non e ancor morto.

[156] *Il Principe*, Chapter 6.

[157] *Traité*, I, 137: "Je dis donc que l'histoire sacrée est ma seule et fidelle guide, mon vray but et mon étoile polaire, à laquelle je vise perpétuellement." Further, de la Noue, *Discours*, 20 f.: "Je cuide qu'il y aura des courtisans qui seront peu satisfaits de mes propos: Mesmes se moqueront de ce que je veux desmesler les affaires d'Estat par des maximes de Theologie: et auroyent plus agreable que celles de Polybe, de Plutarque, et de Xenophon, fussent mises en avant, à fin qu'on jugeast par elles des accidents des Royaumes. J'eusse volontiers appuyé mon dire sur leurs opinions, qui sont tres-belles: mais pour n'estre point abusé, il m'a semblé que la voye que je prenois estoit meilleure: car encor que la sagesse de l'homme (qui lui est toutesfois donnes d'enhaut) reluise aux livres prophane, si est-ce qu'elle est fort vaine, en comparison de la Divine, qui apparoit es Sainctes Escritures."

[158] Compare Bluntschli, *Geschichte der neueren Staatswissenschaft*, p. 29: "Der Hugenottenmord hatte Frankreich weder Ruhe verschafft, noch die Einheit hergestellt. Nur um so heftiger war der konfessionell-politische Zwiespalt wieder ausgebrochen; die fanatische Wut der einen, die Rache der anderen waren noch nicht gesättigt. Die französische Nation war damals in einem ähnlichen selbstmörderischen Zerfleischungsprocesse begriffen wie die deutsche Nation ein halbes Jahrhundert später im ihrem dreissigjährigen Kriege. Die Autorität der Kirche und die Statsordnung schwankten auf dem untergrabenen Fundamente. In einer solchen Zeit sah sich Bodin nach den Rechtsgrundlagen der statlichen Macht um. Wenn es eine Rettung gab, so konnte sie seines Erachtens nur von da aus gefunden werden. Die Machiavellistische Klugheit reichte nicht aus. Eben diese rücksichtlose Wahl auch der schlechtesten, weil fur den Augenblick nützlichen Mittel, zu welchem die Parteiführer allzugeneigt waren, hatten die Nation ins Verderben gestürzt. Mit sittlicher und patriotischer Entrüstung wendet sich daher Bodin gegen Machiavelli." Chauviré in his *Jean Bodin*, p. 271, says, "Le machiavélisme n'avait d'abord été pour nos Français que la théorie d'un fait préexistant, l'anarchie politique et morale; par un choc en retour, il aggravait maintenant

In the politic of Machiavelli tolerance of course found its place; and it is interesting to note in the religious literature of the sixteenth century that what one party regarded as Christian charity was interpreted by the other as Machiavellian duplicity. In the particular case it may indeed be hard to draw the line. "I have marked the state of this neutral government," writes Archbishop Parker to Lord Burghley; "I look for no other end than that is very likely. I have framed myself to be carried away by the floods, when they shall arise. This Machiavel Government is strange to me, for it bringeth forth strange fruits. As soon is the papist favored as is the true protestant."[159] A reply to this sort of attack one may find in John Whitgift's *Defense of the Answer to the Admonition*. One of his opponents had written:—"There is no other thing to be looked for than some speedy vengeance to light upon the whole land provide as well as the politic Machevils think they can, though God do his worst." To this Whitgift replies: "It would be known whom they mean by these 'politic Machevils;' for they envy all men of great authority, wit, and policy."[160] The opposition of the true churchmen to the Machiavellian philosophy of the state is explicit and emphatic enough whatever their critics might say. It is thus that Edwin Sandys expresses himself in one of his sermons:— "Good reason it is that as kings do reign and hold their power by him, so his will revealed in his word, should be the rule and direction of their government. If they think to establish their thrones better by their own wise and politic devices, they are greatly deceived. There is no policy, no wisdom, like the wisdom of God. The commonwealths which Aristotle and Plato have framed in their books, otherwise full of wisdom, yet compared with that city for whose sake and benefit the Lord doth watch, what are they but fancies of foolish men? As for Machiavel's invention they are but the dream of a brain sick person, founded upon the craft of man, and not upon godly wisdom, which only hath good effect."[161] Furthermore, a passage from Thomas Rogers' *Catholic Doctrine of the Church of England* musters as "the adversaries of the Anglicans those who prefer above the scriptures 1. their own inventions, as did the philosophers, whereof one said of Moses, that good man maketh a trim discourse, but proveth nothing; and the Grecians to whom the Gospel is foolishness; 2. their own imagina-

---

cette anarchie, et multipliait, grâce à la louange dont il les entourait, les ruses ou les violences antisociales. D'effet il était devenu cause. Bodin le sentait; il voulait remonter à cette source morale des troubles: le machiavélisme passé dans les têtes, puis dans les moeurs françaises. C'est, pensait-il, la divergence des égoïsmes monstreux développés par de telles doctrines qui dissout le faisceau social: substitutions à cette philosophie la piété, la justice, le dévouement de tous à l'intérêt commun, et les bonnes volontés reformées se chercheront de nouveau, et se reuniront dans une harmonieuse cité."

[159] *Parker Society*, XXVII, 391.
[160] *Works (Parker Society)*, Division 3, p. 508.
[161] *Parker Society*, XLVI, p. 153.

tions, as did the Manichees, David George, and do the Turks, and Family of Love; 3. or traditions as do the Papists, who more cruelly do punish the violaters of their own traditions and ordinances, than they do the breakers of God's commandments; 4. or statutes, edicts, judgments, proclamations, etc. proceeding from the brain of man; as Machiavel doth, and his scholars."[162]

To every good Protestant in the time of Spenser Machiavel and his scholars were associated particularly with the adherents of the Catholic cause. This was due in part to the terrorism and the intrigue with which the Guises promoted Catholic interests in France. When the Huguenot Coligny was on his way to Paris, he was "beset by letters which reminded him of the queen mother's crooked ways, and the detestable education of the king trained in every sort of violence and horrible sin; his Bible is Machiavelli; he has been prepared by the blood of beasts for the shedding of human blood; he has been persuaded that a prince is not bound to observe an edict extorted by his subjects."[162a] I might cite too a declaration of one Henry Young on August 16, 1594 in relation to Jesuit plots in England (*C.S.P. Domestic Series*, vol. 3):—"England is governed by the Machiavellian policy of those who would be kings and whom it is time to cut off." Baudrillart is clearly correct in declaring in his volume *Bodin et son Temps* that Machiavellism among its leaders, fanaticism both exalted and miserable among the masses, was the true spirit of the Holy League.[163]

It should be conceded, however, that the word Machiavellian in the sixteenth century was a pretty general term of reproach that went, as Montaigne says, like a bird of passage from one party to another. To the bigot the tolerant were Machiavellian because they seemed to sacrifice principle to expediency. So Duke Casimir as reported in a letter from Daniel Rogers to Walsingham under date of October 5, 1577, said, "he would not trust the king of Navarre because of 'machiavilliards' which were about him" (*State Papers, Foreign*, 1577–1578, p. 229). On the other hand, the Jesuits, as we have just remarked, bore a similar reproach because in the administration of the Society of Jesus they seemed to have put into practise that unscrupulous doctrine of force and efficiency of which Machiavelli is the most celebrated expounder. However variously the term might have been applied it was very generally one of reproach; so that it seems to me improbable that the poet of the *Faerie Queene*, whatever might have been his admiration of the *Prince*, the *Discorsi*, and the *History of Florence* (and who indeed can withhold admiration from the literary

---

[162] *Parker Society*, XLV, p. 79.

[162a] Guizot, *Popular History of France*, vol. IV, p. 361.

[163] Baudrillart, *op. cit.*, p. 96. The Latin edition of the Anti-Machiavel, 1577, declares that the English are fortunate in not having been afflicted with Machiavellism:—"Vos vero ô quam fortunatos cum tali Regina, tum quod pestilens Machiavellicae doctrinae afflatus in Angliam non penetravit." It will be remembered that it is the Duke D'Alençon to whom the French edition of 1576 was dedicated. Compare *English Historical Review*, IV, 17, Note.

achievement in these works?), would have based his defense of Lord Grey upon what must have been for him a largely discredited theory of the State. He was writing in the spirit of the most enlightened Anglican thought and of that closely related body of French speculation which was openly anti-Machiavellian. It is, indeed, against Machiavellian duplicity and violence in the persons of Archimago, Duessa, Dolon, Grantorto, that the heroes of the *Faerie Queene* fight the battles of God; and in the following stanza I think we have an explicit arraignment of Machiavellism:

> O sacred hunger of ambitious mindes,
> And impotent desire of men to raine!
> Whom neither dread of God, that devils bindes,
> Nor lawes of men that common-weales containe,
> Nor bands of nature that wilde beastes restraine,
> Can keepe from outrage and from doing wrong,
> Where they may hope a kingdome to obtaine:
> No faith so firme, no trust can be so strong,
> No love so lasting then, that may enduren long.
> *F. Q.* V, XII, St. 1.

For myself I can find no sharper antithesis than that between Spenser and Machiavelli. To the Machiavellian duplicity, Spenser opposes a confident reliance upon righteousness; to *virtu* he opposes virtue; to statecraft he opposes a philosophy of justice; and instead of resting his polity upon lessons of efficiency independently drawn from human disaster and success, he bases it squarely upon a philosophy of justice that derives from the teachings of Christ and the formulated wisdom of the ancient world. The genius of Spenser was, indeed, essentially spiritual; that of Machiavelli, scientific. The one sought by an astonishing effort of the synthetic imagination to weave a gorgeous tapestry of Christian thought and pagan morality, of mediaeval imagery and humanistic ideas, that would be a pattern of human conduct and of true courtesy. The other by a no less astonishing effort of the analytic faculty tried to draught from human experience a code manual of *realpolitik*. The one transmits an accumulated culture of the spirit; the other searches the human record for the secret of efficiency and the key of success.

INDEX

Alençon, 34, 39.
Anti-Machiavel, 39.
Bacon, Francis, 19 ff.
Bodin, Jean, 33 ff., 48 f., 51 ff.
But de la guerre et de la paix, 26 note 49.
Discours politiques et militaires, 31 ff.
Du Bellay, 7.
Faerie Queene, 7 ff., 51, 53 ff., 74.
Grey, Arthur, 10 ff., 63.
Grosart, Alexander B., 10.
Harvey, Gabriel, 21 f., 34, 48 ff.
Henry of Navarre, 23, 29.
Hooker, Richard, 17.
Jewell, John, 160 ff.
Languet, Huebert, 50.
La None, François de, 31 ff., 49 f.
L'Hôpital, Michel de, 25 ff., 49 note 129.
Machiavelli, 64 ff.

Martin Marprelate, 17.
Methodus ad facilem historiarum cognitionem, 34, 35 ff., 60 f., 62.
Montaigne, 26.
Montesquieu, 35.
Parker, Matthew, 72.
Princeps Christianus, 69.
Rogers, Daniel, 73.
Rogers, Thomas, 72 f.
Sandys, Edwin, 72.
Satyre, Ménippée, 23 ff.
Seneca, 29 f.
Six Livres de la République, 38 ff., 50 ff.
Traité de la Reformation de Justice, 26 ff.
Veue of the Present State of Ireland, 51 ff., 57 ff.
Whitgift, John, 17 f., 72.